Custom Cars
Coupes ■ Sedans ■ Pickups

Alan Mayes

motorbooks

Dedication

This book is dedicated to Geno DiPol, *Ol' Skool Rodz* and *Car Kulture DeLuxe* publisher, my good friend, colleague, and business partner.

First published in 2010 by Motorbooks, an imprint of MBI Publishing Company, 400 First Avenue North, Suite 300, Minneapolis, MN 55401 USA

Copyright © 2010 by MBI Publishing Company

Motorbooks titles are also available at discounts in bulk quantity for industrial or sales-promotional use. For details write to Special Sales Manager at MBI Publishing Company, 400 First Avenue North, Suite 300, Minneapolis, MN 55401 USA.

To find out more about our books, visit us online at www.motorbooks.com.

ISBN-13: 978-0-7603-3760-8

Editor: Peter Schletty
Design Manager: John Sticha
Designed by: Kazuko Collins

Printed in China

Contents

Introduction

"**C**ustom cars"—the term sends the thoughts of many a gearhead racing. Oh, there are people who don't care for customs. Their favorite cars are hot rods, restored classics, street rods, or muscle cars. Nothing wrong with that. I've owned some of each of those over the years. Those cars just don't inspire the imagination like a custom, though. Customs are rolling works of art, and their builders are the artists.

There are only so many things you can do with a hot rod to make it unique. Think not? Go to the Street Rod Nationals sometime and try to explain the differences among the dozens of red Deuce roadsters with black interiors you'll see. And if you've seen one restored 1965 Chevelle SS, you've pretty much seen them all. Ah, but customs, that's a different matter. Except for the few clones of the more famous iconic customs of the early years, no two are alike. That's why they're called "customs" after all!

Customs have been my favorite type of modified cars for at least 50 years. When I was a kid in little Daleville, Indiana, Johnson's Store (in the middle of town at the only stoplight) carried the digest-sized custom car magazines on its newsstand. That's where my meager allowance went every week for a few years . . . except when it went for model cars.

Back then (in the late 1950s/early 1960s), AMT and Jo-Han annually released plastic three-in-one kits of the latest Detroit iron. AMT did Fords and most of the GM products. Jo-Han did the Chrysler and AMC offerings, plus Cadillac and Oldsmobile. Though the parts were included in the kits to build "stock, race, or custom," I always built custom. Always. Several decades later, I'm still playing with customs, although my wife wishes it were those 1/25-scale plastic models.

When I go to a car show like the Detroit Autorama, the Grand National Roadster Show, the Road

1 No customizers have ever made more tasteful cars than the Alexander Brothers from Detroit. They (Mike and Larry) always built their cars with impeccable proportions and execution, never overdone. The 1956 Chevy, *Golden Chariot*, is owned by Lou Calasibetta, who also restored the car at his Old Stillwater Garage in Stillwater, New Jersey. Lou's craftsmanship is on a par with the best, including the A-Brothers, so it's fitting he has the car.

2 Dave Kinnaman (of Kinnaman's Kustom Kars) of the Anderson, Indiana, area built this 1939 Ford custom in the 1980s. Now owned by Texan John Spencer, the car is a great example of a traditional-style custom with its Carson-style top, Packard grille (a popular upgrade for 1930s to 1940s cars in the Harry Westergard style), whitewalls, and single bar flipper wheel covers.

Rocket Rumble, or the Sacramento Autorama, it's still the customs that attract my attention. I appreciate the cool hot rods and all the other cars, understand, but customs are my first love. Other than the newer daily drivers for my wife and me, the cars in our garages are all customs. One's finished, one's a project, one's next in line. And to be honest, I'm living the dream: what is sometimes called by those immersed in it "the kustom lifestyle." My day job is being the managing editor for *Car Kulture DeLuxe* and *Ol' Skool Rodz* magazines. I'm surrounded by customs and hot rods all the time. I get paid to talk about, write about, and photograph customs and hot rods.

For want of a better term, I guess you could say I'm a purist when it comes to custom cars. Only American cars make good customs, and of those, it's cars between about 1936 and the mid-1960s that make the best. The choice of good custom fodder is a matter of a car's original style and there were not clear industry-wide demarcations regarding styling updates. For instance, 1936 is about the time that most cars wore what we now refer to as "fat fenders," a feature that lends itself well to customization techniques, such as fadeaway fenders, seam removal, and other smoothing procedures. However, some cars had the style in 1935, and others got better style in 1937. On the opposite end, General Motors' full-sized cars through about 1966 lend themselves well to customizing. Go beyond that and the cars started getting too big and ugly on the outside and too plasticky on the inside. Of course, there are exceptions to every rule, even unwritten ones. I've seen a few attractive customs newer than 1966. Very few. Most of them should have been left stock. The time and effort would have been better spent on a more suitable, older candidate.

Which brings me to some specifics about what I think looks good on a custom car and some standards that I believe should be applied to the building of a custom. These aren't really rules, of course, but they should be. Some I'll mention here; others I'll save for later chapters.

Custom cars should be low. Cars have always been customized to make them sleeker. That includes sitting low. If you're building the car a little at a time as you drive it, lower it first. It doesn't take long, and it will make a huge difference in the way the car looks. It will inspire you for the rest of the project. Nothing else you do will look right until the car is lowered. And it should either sit level or a little bit higher in the front than in the back. The other way around looks goofy.

Customization should be an upgrade, always moving up in status and year. No recognizable Chevy parts on a custom Cadillac or Oldsmobile. No Studebaker parts on a Lincoln. No 1939 parts on a 1951 car. When using production car parts, the rule of thumb is newer and/or higher in status;

otherwise build custom parts. But the production car parts shouldn't be *too* new. They should be within a specific period of only a few years newer than the car. Less than ten for sure, maybe less than five. Otherwise, you wind up mixing styles that don't work together. Example: Lay back-style 1990s Mercedes headlights on a 1940s or 1950s car look stupid. Sorry, but they do. It's too much of a jump in styles.

Whitewall tires belong on every custom, and here's why: Customizing a car is the act of upgrading it in style and stature. That includes adding whitewall tires appropriate in style to the year of the car. A car is not customized to add a performance image or utility. That means that cars styled up through about 1960 should always have wide whitewalls—not

3 Oz Customs in Oroville, California, has built several cars for John D'Agostino, one of the most active custom car personalities around. D'Agostino commissions a new car almost every year, and all of them are as beautiful as this 1957 Oldsmobile. He has "the eye" and always designs a car that is subtly customized, built as though the manufacturer could have—and should have—built it that way.

4 Famed customizer Darryl Starbird bought a brand new Buick in 1959 and then took it to his Star Custom Shop in Wichita and restyled it. This is the result, as it appeared in magazines in 1960. Starbird now owns and operates Darryl Starbird's National Rod & Custom Hall of Fame Museum in Afton, Oklahoma. He also produces car shows in the Midwest and builds cars for those shows and the museum.

5 Gordy Brown, of Centerville, Utah, no longer builds cars for customers, but he has several of his own and he's been into customs since he was a kid. Here's his 1954 Ford Skyliner (with see-through top), which he says is very much like one he had in high school. He's even planning to leave it in spotted primer to recall that original car.

6 This 1956 Mercury is a mild custom, showing how just a little bit of work can transform a car. Extraneous chrome trim has been removed, as have the door handles. The car is lowered and not much else. Cars from the mid-1950s had *lots* of chrome trim and often just strategically removing some of it makes a huge difference in the appearance of the car.

7 Customs are about class, and nothing says class more than a 1950s Cadillac. Such cars also require a lot of planning to be able to pull off a successful customization. This one has received work that tastefully exaggerates its stock features. The fins have been extended and the top chopped, both operations accenting each other.

blackwalls, not white letters, not redlines. Narrower whitewalls were available at tire stores in 1961 and became available on production cars in 1962. Whitewalls, that's the rule.

Don't mix styles. If you want a pro street car for some perverted, inexplicable reason, build it. But please, *please*, don't try to make a custom part pro street or part muscle car, or part hot rod. It never works. And billet parts have no part on a custom car—ever. Billet is chunky and ugly, and it does not say "custom." It says . . . well, never mind what it says. Billet is the anticustom. It should be forever exorcised from any custom car.

Of all the different kinds of modified cars in our world, customs are the most individualistic, the most expressive of their owner's (or builder's) personality and taste. Cer-

tain custom car designers or builders commission a new car nearly every year, every one of which is gorgeous. John D'Agostino, Richard Zocchi, and Rick Dore come to mind. A few of their cars are shown in this book's chapters. Others of us build, or have built, one custom in a lifetime. It's the one and only dream car. The rest of us are somewhere in between and might have a few custom cars over our lifetimes.

The purpose of this book is to show you some ways that other builders have expressed themselves in their cars. We'll show you some beautiful cars and offer some ideas for building a custom. We hope you'll use this as a reference and that it will inspire you to some new ideas of your own, some ideas that will make your car uniquely yours. Let's turn some pages.

8

9

10

11

8 Chevy Fleetline fastback sedans (and the similarly styled Pontiacs and Oldsmobiles) make very sleek customs. Because of the smooth, long flow of their rooflines extending into the rear deck, they can be challenging cars to chop. Done correctly like this one, though, they are gorgeous.

9 The *Golden Indian* was another beautiful Alexander Brothers creation, a somewhat futuristic take on the gorgeous-from-the-factory 1960 Pontiac. This car is owned and was restored by Lou Calasibetta of Old Stillwater Garage.

10 Among the most popular customizing subject cars are 1949 to 1951 Mercurys. This one was built by Bo Huff of Bo Huff Customs in East Carbon, Utah. It belongs to his sister and her husband. While many custom builders are content to do the same style top chop over and over on Mercurys of the era, Bo Huff does each one differently. Like all Bo Huff customs, this one has wide whitewall tires.

11 Buicks like this 1956 are good examples of the style of cars that it's easy to mess up if you try to do too much to them. Thankfully, that's not the case here. A simple nosing/decking/shaving (removal of chrome on the hood, trunk, and elsewhere, respectively), along with the addition of a tube grille and Skylark-style wire wheels make for a very classy car.

12–14 When planning a custom car build, it's sometimes a good idea to take some straight-on shots of the car and just do some cut-and-paste customization with paper cutouts. It's cheap and easy and will allow you to experiment with different chops, channels, lowering height, etc. The same thing can be done with Photoshop, but paper is cheaper and easier to do.

15 Another way to visualize how a car will look is to have an artist like the super-talented Jeff Allison do a concept drawing like this one he did of an early 1950s Studebaker for *Ol' Skool Rodz* magazine several years ago.

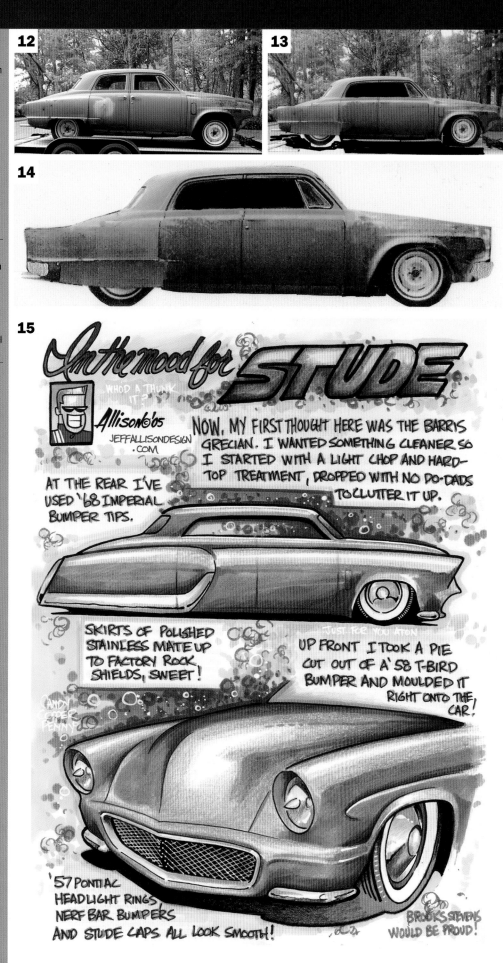

Chapter 1
Prewar Cars

Though a few cars could be considered "customs" before that time, it wasn't until the Art Deco movement and its accompanying Streamline Moderne style of industrial design made it into mainstream automobiles that customizing really took off. We mark 1936 as the beginning of this period of car styles that lend themselves so well to customization, though in some makes the 1935 models are very similar.

The mid-1930s marked the end of the Great Depression, and Americans were treated to new, more streamlined cars, especially by the Big Three Detroit automakers. The boxy styles of the 1920s and early 1930s were superseded by stylish streamlining. These cars—often referred to as "fat fendered" by street rodders—provided fodder for talented customizers, such as the Barris brothers, Bill Hines, Harry Westergard, and many others, to

take a common used Chevrolet, Ford, or Buick and make it as stylish as a more expensive Packard or Cadillac. Customizers applied fadeaway fenders, chopped Carson-style tops, and used tail-dragging lowered stances to make some of the most beautiful cars ever seen.

Produced from about 1935 through 1946, or up to 1948 depending on make (and minus 1943 to 1945 for World War II), these cars were plentiful, and they were the raw canvas of thousands of customs well up into the early 1950s.

This style of car is still popular today, and many customizers of all ages ply their trade on these types of cars. Though the raw material in good condition is getting harder and harder to find, some cars of this span remain available, and companies such as EMS Automotive, Bob Drake Reproductions, Bitchin' Products, and Chevs of the 1940s make replacement sheetmetal panels for Fords and Chevrolets of the era.

1 and 2 When Bill Cushenbery built *El Matador* in the early 1960s, it was one of the wildest custom prewar Fords ever. Harold Murphy fell in love with the car back then. Years later he owned it, but in the meantime it had been almost completely destroyed in a garage fire. He and Mike Scott (together, the team of Murphy & the Striper) and friends restored the car. *El Matador* reflects the early 1960s in style and Cushenbery's excellent craftsmanship. Virtually every square inch of it was customized. It took someone with Harold Murphy's affinity for the car to be able to pull off a restoration from the burned-out and rusty hulk he started with.

3 Here's an example of why the Barris brothers were held in such high regard in the early days of customs. This is a Bill Hines–built clone of the 1940 Mercury that the Barris shop built for Nick Matranga in 1949. More than 50 years later, it is still the most influential early Mercury of all time, having been cloned and near-cloned many times.

4 The influence of the Matranga Mercury can be seen here in Fip Buchanan's pretty 1940 Merc. Every seam has been smoothed, and the car is as slick as they come. Powered by a 302 Ford and running Air Ride suspension, it's a worthy highway hauler too. Note the curved side windows similar to the Matranga Merc.

5

6

7

8

9

5 and 6 This Ford, once owned by Jack Stewart, started life as a 1941 business coupe and was finished in the Barris shop in Lynwood, California. It was in *Motor Life* magazine in 1954. Its grille is made up of 1949 Cadillac components. The car is chopped, channeled, and sectioned. When it was chopped, the windshield was moved up into the roof to facilitate better driver vision. The Ford was involved in a very serious accident after being sold to a man in Ohio. Indiana resident Bob Drake spotted it on a tow truck being taken to a junkyard. He bought it and restored it. He owned it when these photos were taken, but he has since sold it.

7 This is Darryl Starbird's 1947 Cadillac, the car that brought him national attention. Cars such as this make very classy customs, especially done Starbird-style with miles-deep black paint, wire wheels, and whitewalls. It was shaved and molded but not chopped. Headlights are from a 1958 Chevy.

8 Fords from 1935 and 1936 have long been popular custom material. They're fairly plentiful, at least compared to other cars of the same years, and respond well to chopping, lowering, and two-tone paint schemes. Packard-style grilles are a popular swap too. This one has blackwall tires. Most customs have whitewalls these days.

9 See why 1936 Fords are so popular as customs? Fender skirts, a low stance, and the right paint and accoutrements and they're really hard to beat. This three-window style is more popular than the five-window version in the previous photo because of its smooth, flowing design.

10 Not to be overlooked are mid-1930s Mopar coupes—Plymouths, Dodges, DeSotos, and Chryslers. Every bit as stylish as competing brands, they translate well into customs and they're less commonly used as customs, so they are more unique.

11 Dave Kinnaman of Kinnaman's Kustom Kars in Alexandria, Indiana, originally built this 1939 Ford custom convertible. The Packard grille was added by a subsequent owner. With its chopped Carson-style top, lowered stance, smooth flowing lines, and whitewalls with flipper hubcaps, the car shows the classic profile.

12 Pretty clean and tasteful straight from the factory, Cadillacs like this Sedanette (a fastback sedan) don't require a ton of work. This one's been lowered; the door handles and most of the chrome emblems have been removed, but the simple side spear remains. Later chrome Caddy wire wheels are a classy touch, as is the dark solid color.

13 Similar in style to the Cadillacs, Buick Sedanettes also make big, stylish customs. This one has modified 1950s Cadillac front bumpers, as well as hooded headlights. It's chopped and has the Matranga Merc–style side window treatment.

14 Here's another Buick done in a different style. It obviously has air suspension since it's sitting on the ground. Molded-in sidepipes, Buick portholes, and spotlights are the only chrome on the suede green body. Wheel treatment includes simple Shannon cones and trim rings on body-color steel wheels.

15 If you hear someone mention a car being done "Westergard-style," this is an example of what he or she is often referring to. The convertibles will have a Carson-style top and the car will sit low, but not so low as to be bothersome to drive. It'll often be dark red or a similar dark color. The front end will be reworked, though not always in a way considered universally attractive. The chop and profile will be near perfect.

16 Believe it or not, this car is a 1936 Ford. It has been completely transformed, though whether for the better is certainly up for debate. A 1936 Ford is a beautiful car to begin with, so any custom work needs to be done sparingly and tastefully. Willys and Cadillac parts are identifiable here.

17 An extremely beautiful custom 1940 Mercury with work done by two of the masters: Dick Bertolucci and Harry Westergard. The grille is one of the cleanest ever put in a production car, the 1946 Chevy. The car has been flawlessly restored and was photographed at the Sacramento Autorama.

18 This smooth 1938 Ford sedan has been a multiple winner at East Coast shows. It utilizes nerf bars instead of a front bumper, but it does have a rear bumper. The car was tastefully chopped and the B-pillar removed. Side window frames are slanted. Classic paint scallops accentuate the body lines without drawing undue attention to the paint itself.

19 This 1940 Mercury is a fine example of a mild custom. It's chopped a little, shaved a little, and lowered a little. That makes for a comfortably drivable car. It's running radial wide whitewalls with flipper wheel covers on the steel rims. Stock bumpers are retained as is the nice Mercury horizontal bar grille.

20 Built by Oz Customs in Oroville, California, Brian Everett's 1940 Mercury is breathtaking from any angle. Its B-pillars are removed, making a hardtop. The top is radically chopped and the lines flow just right. Dual spotlights and chrome reverse wheels give a nod to tradition. Note the molded-in bullets where the bumper brackets used to be.

21 Here's another clean, mild custom Mopar product. The tasteful medium green color, ivory wheels, and full smooth wheel covers do nothing to belie the era in which the car was truly built. It could have been 1951 or 2001.

22 Richard Zocchi's 1939 Dodge coupe is as smooth as they come. It's been customized from one end to the other and has a great flowing top chop, a molded-in LaSalle grille, and slightly canted dual headlights. Running boards were retained and molded into the fenders.

23 and 24 Believe it or not, these are both 1940 Chevys! Does a better example of what customization can do for a car exist? The green car has been given the smoothing custom treatment. Fenders and running boards are seamlessly molded, and there's a Cadillac grille. Bumpers are tucked in tightly and molded in as well. The top is chopped, and the B-pillar has been replaced with curved window frames. By contrast, the orange car is more of a hot rod, with no hood, and it's neither molded nor chopped.

25 Here's a 1941 Lincoln coupe from Finland. Larger than Mercurys or Fords of the period, the Lincolns still have the Ford family look but in a sleeker, elongated style. This one has fender skirts and the top has been chopped. The grille is stock, and why not? It's a great design.

26 The 1940 Coachcraft Mercury, now owned by Derby Ahlstone. Built by Coachcraft of Hollywood in the early 1950s, it had been sitting for years when Ahlstone bought it. The list of parts of the car not customized would be shorter than the list of custom touches.

27 Larry Grobe's *Voodoo Idol* 1946 Ford coupe was built as a tribute to his custom car idol, Gene Winfield. It was chopped, channeled, and sectioned. The grille is from a 1947 Studebaker and the bumpers are from a 1949 Caddy. They have Kaiser overriders. The hood was handmade because Larry couldn't find one he liked.

28 Ron Gomez addressed the main styling flaw with cars like his 1941 Buick: the top height. He chopped it four inches, bringing the whole car into a smoother design flow. Continuing to smooth, he recessed the pretty Buick grille and Frenched the headlights. He also molded the fenders and running boards to the body.

29

30

31

29 Here's a late 1940s Plymouth that looks great. The hood has been brought to a point above the 1946 Chevy grille. Wheel covers are from a 1953 Studebaker. The front bumper is molded in tightly, and the fender skirts have "speed lines" that match the ones in the fenders. Fenders and running boards are molded.

30 This late 1940s Chevy was styled after the *High School Confidential* movie cars by its builder, Dave Pareso of Back Street Kustoms in Colorado. That included filling in the rear quarter windows to make the coupe into a three-window. The top was chopped and ribbed DeSoto bumpers were added snugly against the front gravel pan.

31 This 1949 Plymouth P-15 (carryover 1946 to 1948 style) convertible has it all: Buick headlights, a Kaiser-style grille, a Carson top, molded fenders front and rear, and ribbed bumpers. The interior colors mimic the exterior, making for an attractive and bright custom cruiser.

32 and 33 This 1946 Chevy is a smooth eye-grabber. The fastback Chevy has been nicely chopped, and the flow of the top is perfection. B-pillars were removed to give the car a hardtop look, and the vent windows were taken out as well. Front fenders were molded back into fadeaways, flowing into the rear fenders. The windshield is v-butted, and the grille opening is made of two upper 1946 openings fastened together to form an oval. The flawless dark green metallic paint accentuates the air of class.

34 This 1941 Cadillac Sedanette is a drivable work in progress, illustrating the wisdom of driving a car as it is being completed. The downside is that sometimes the owner is having so much fun driving the car that he never stops long enough to work on it. That's not all bad either.

35 and 36 Here's another 1940s Caddy in progress. The owner sold this one to finance another car purchase so he didn't get to see it through. However, it has the makings of a knockout beauty. The top is chopped and made into a three-window coupe. The grille is from a 1952 Cadillac and the bumper bullet sections are from a 1954 Caddy.

37 Except for the chopped top and the olds Fiesta wheel covers, this 1941 Ford coupe from Colorado is mostly stock. Additional modifications include a louvered hood and Frenched headlights.

38 On the other hand, this 1941 Ford coupe, also a Colorado car, is heavily modified. Chopped, hardtopped, molded, smoothed, and wearing molded-in sidepipes, it's radically different from the preceding red 1941. The bumpers were removed and the car was given rolled pans in their place.

39 and 40 Metallica's James Hetfield owns this 1937 Ford coupe dubbed *The Crimson Ghost*. Rick Dore commissioned the build. Like most Rick Dore customs, it has smooth, flowing styling with lots of little mods the average person won't see without being told what to look for.

1

Chapter 2
1949–1951 Fords & Mercurys

Mercurys from 1949 to 1951 have long been the most popular cars to be customized. Blame Sam Barris. Half of the well-known and highly regarded Barris brothers, Sam bought a brand new 1949 Mercury and immediately chopped it. Sam's customizing skills and tastes are now legendary, and 60 years later, customizers still consider it to be a perfect Merc chop. It's the one against which all others are judged.

James Dean (and the lovely Natalie Wood) added to the custom Merc mystique inadvertently through their association with one of the

cars in the movie *Rebel Without a Cause*. The fact that Dean preferred sports cars and motorcycles is lost on the Dean Mercury faithful. The James Dean Run car show, held each September in Dean's hometown of Fairmount, Indiana, features a Mercurys-only section called "The Merc Corral."

Very nearly as popular, and much more plentiful, are the 1949 to 1951 Shoebox Fords, so called because of their more rectangular shape as compared to the bulbous 1941 to 1948 Fords that preceded them. The 1949 Ford's appearance was very modern for the time, with the

1 Here's a great example of why Shoebox Fords are popular as customs. Charlie Schmidt's 1951 coupe utilizes 1955 Chevy headlights, 1954 Chevy parking lights on the Ford grille, chrome reverse wheels with spiders, and two-tone paint separated by a combination of 1951 Ford and 1957 Chevy trim.

2 Murphy & the Striper (Harold Murphy and Mike Scott) built this cool Shoebox Ford several years ago. It has DeSoto grille teeth, Frenched headlights, and Oldsmobile side trim. The stance is just right, as is the top chop with angled B-pillars. The fender skirts are teardrop style.

3 The rear of the same Ford shows tunneled blue-dot 1959 Cadillac taillights set into the Ford's existing taillight fender bulges, a good example of using the car's features to custom advantage. The dummy lakes pipes are the three-outlet style. The radio antenna is sunken.

4 This copper mild custom 1950 Ford is the kind that would make a great daily driver. For less than the cost of a new Camry or Impala, this car could be built with a dependable modern V-8, overdrive automatic transmission, and Vintage Air heat/cool/defrost.

5 Michael Shea from Kansas owns this Ford, which utilizes parts from all three years of the Shoebox era. It has tasteful scallops in a traditional style and a great stance and chop. A single floating grille bar complements the chrome on the hood.

hoods being almost flush with the fender tops and its overall smooth, sleek styling.

Mercurys and Fords from 1949 to 1951 make wonderful customs. Mechanically, they are very similar, and since they are from the same manufacturer and span the same three years, we've grouped them together in this chapter. Lincolns from the same period fit the mold as well.

6 Here's another tasty coupe, a 1949 Ford built by Bo Huff Customs in Utah. It's shaved, nosed, decked, and lowered. Cars like this reflect the great job that Ford Motor Company stylists did in designing the 1949 to 1951 Fords to start with. They provided a great foundation.

7 New Jersey customizer Adrian Jacquet did about everything that could be done to his 1949 Ford coupe. It's chopped, sectioned, lowered on an Air Ride system, and painted red metalflake. The teardrop skirts were originally intended for a Mercury.

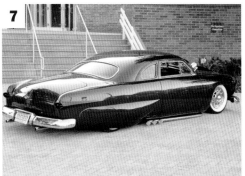

8 Jacquet's coupe also has a single floating grille bar, a sun visor, a louvered hood, and tri-tip lakes pipes. Wheel covers are from a mid-1950s Cadillac. The interior is metalflake vinyl.

9 This 1951 Ford Victoria has a bit of an East Coast flair in its rake (the front is lower than the back). It also sports 1955 Pontiac side trim and a narrowed 1955 DeSoto grille.

10 The work on Wayne Jones' red 1951 Ford spans several decades. The car was originally customized in the 1950s, but it was chopped and painted in the 1980s. It wears canted headlights and a bar grille. Rolled pans replaced the bumpers. Wayne hails from Noblesville, Indiana.

11 Wearing suede maroon paint and wide whites on chrome steel wheels, this 1949 Ford sedan looks like it could have been on the road in this form in the 1950s. Two giveaways are its current aftermarket Briz ribbed bumpers and V-butted windshield. This is a practical cruiser, chopped conservatively.

12 Here's a nicely chopped 1951 Ford Victoria. The side trim is a combination from a couple of different cars. The grille is from a 1954 DeSoto. Extended rear fenders house Packard taillights. The headlights are Frenched. Note the rear wheelwells are opened to match the fronts.

13 This seriously chopped and flamed 1949 can be seen running all over Southern California. Note the ride height; lower than stock but reasonable enough to make for mostly scrape-free driving.

14 The narrowed 1957 Chevy front bumper gives this green Shoebox a completely different look. The square tube bar grille is another tasty addition, as are the Oldsmobile headlights. The wheel covers are from a Cadillac.

15

16

17

18

19

15 During its chop, this sedan surrendered its B-pillar and now has a hardtop style. Note the 1954 Chevy grille, a popular swap. Barely visible through the windows are the 1964 Thunderbird wraparound rear seats.

16 Here's a genuine 1950s-style custom Ford coupe. The side trim is from a 1957 DeSoto. The grille is a combination of an Olds grille bar and 1949 to 1950 Mercury. The rear fins are from the mind of the builder.

17 This very conservative 1951 coupe has simply been nosed and decked and lowered. Lancer four-bar hubcaps and a slight lowering result in a simple, tasteful car.

18 Drive 'em while you build 'em—that's the unspoken message conveyed by the owner of this East Coast 1949 sedan. Note the retained tall header over the windshield and the chop that tapers slightly toward the rear. The wheel coves are 1961 Buick.

19 Chuck Fisher built this 1949 coupe, and it has 50 body mods, including extended suicide doors, canted 1958 Lincoln headlights, a grille made of two handmade bars, and handmade bumpers. The car is now a three-window coupe, and the top is chopped 3 1/2 inches. It also has custom fender covers in front and rear.

20 Ford Victorias from 1951 are so pretty that some guys just remove some emblems and door handles and let their paint jobs do the talking. Here's one such example. Lancer hubcaps on the requisite red steel wheels, whitewall tires, and a 1950s-style scallop paint job work well together.

21 Well, here it is, the Mercury that launched a thousand (or more) customs. Sam Barris chopped this 1949 right after he brought it home from the new car dealer. Roy Brizio's shop recently restored it for current owner John Mumford. This is the benchmark for Mercury chops.

22 This is undoubtedly the best-known custom Mercury of all time: the Barris Brothers-built Hirohata. Bob Hirohata drove the car from California to Indianapolis in 1953 for a custom car show. It won. The perfect proportions on the Hirohata Merc are another nod to Sam Barris' skill and taste.

23 Joe Bailon, creator of Candy Apple paint, built this Merc four-door and made a convertible out of it. It has a lift-off, Carson-style top. The grille uses 1954 Chevy teeth. The wheel covers are three-bar spinners.

24 Here's another Bailon Mercury. This one shows his more flamboyant style with its scooped, pancaked, and peaked hood. Note the rectangular covers on the front fenders, four-bar tubular custom bumpers, and reverse hooded headlights. The grille bar is from a 1956 Plymouth, and the paint is flawless, mile-deep Candy Apple Maroon.

25 Bo Huff of East Carbon, Utah, is a prolific Mercury custom builder. Though he's chopped dozens, he tries to never chop two alike. This black 1951 appears mostly stock except for the chop. It retains most of its stock trim and isn't even very low.

26 Another Bo Huff Mercury, this one belongs to Bo's sister and her husband. The B-pillars are slightly angled, and the top flows smoothly toward the rear. Note the twin antennas in the doors. The wheel covers are genuine 1956 Olds Fiestas.

27 One of the most sought-after Mercury top choppers was Dick Dean. He passed away in 2008, and Jeff Neppl has the distinction of owning this 1949 Merc, the last one Dean chopped. The car was featured in both *Car Kulture DeLuxe* and *Kustoms Illustrated* magazines.

28 Though this car started life as a 1950 Mercury, it has pieces of several different cars now. The top is from a 1952 Buick, and the hood, fenders, and rear quarters are part the original car, part later Mercury, and part Buick. The car was started in 1954 and finished in 1957. It has no parts newer than 1956 and still runs six-volt electrics.

29 Mike Lanning's stunning yellow and white 1951 Mercury would be just as attention-getting in a more subdued hue. It wears the always popular 1953 Buick side trim, and the fender fadeaways follow the same contour. Rear fenders are toothed and scooped, and the grille is a DeSoto with extra teeth. The stance and top chop are perfect.

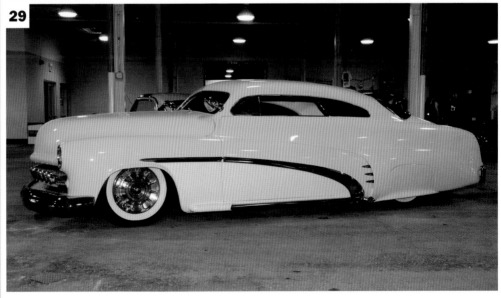

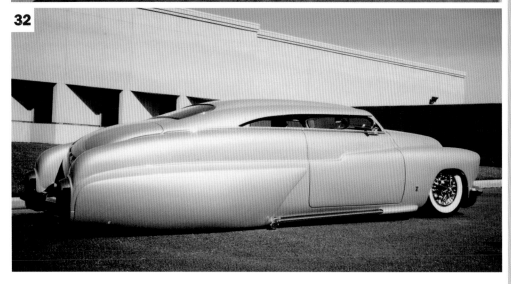

30 Hardtopped, chopped, V-butted, scooped, and lowered, this suede green Mercury is hard to ignore. It's a road burner too.

31 Bill Wolf's 1950 *California Gold* is a re-creation of a car that the legendary Gene Winfield built in the 1960s. Winfield built the clone too. Molded sidepipes, Chrysler grille bars, and Buick headlights are accented by Winfield's gold candy paint and scallops.

32 Gary "Chopit" Fioto created this 1951 Merc for a customer who originally just wanted his sagging doors fixed. The fastback top utilizes a center section from a Chevy Fleetline. The rear bumper ends/taillights are from a 1960 Cadillac. Chopit custom made the huge teardrop fender skirts.

33 Gary "Chopit" Fioto tends to modernize his Mercury builds rather than following a strict traditional style. This long and low 1951 convertible is a good example of how well that works for him. The proportions are excellent, and the mid-1950s Cadillac front bumper and Packard taillights add to the visual impact.

34 East Coast style again, *Misty Blue* is a regular trophy winner at the Lead East car show in New Jersey. It has a ribbed rolled pan, single bar grille, and Frenched headlights. Note the car's name lettered on the front fender.

35 A rear view of *Misty Blue* shows off the Carson-style convertible top with the small back window, Frenched taillights, and another ribbed rolled pan. This is a good example of continuity between front and rear. The front fenders are notched for the lakes pipes.

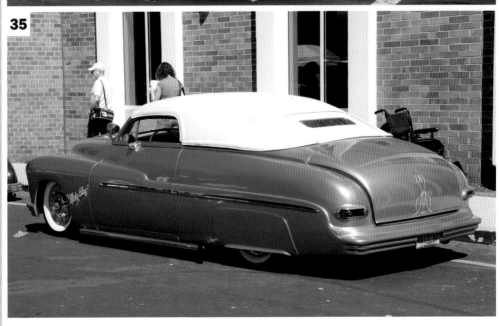

36 There's a lot going on with this chopped and hardtopped Mercury. The side trim is from a 1954 to 1956 Buick, and the single bar grille has teeth on the top only. The headlights are Frenched 1954 Buick items above 1955 Pontiac bumpers on a rolled pan. The side pipes with triple outlets are molded in and scallop-molded halfway back. Purple with flames too, this one's wild.

37 This Merc is a little more modern-conservative. The wheelwells are open, and the tasteful bullet grille is above a gravel pan molded closely over the bumper. Removed B-pillars, hood louvers, and speed line–style scallops lend a sporty air to this one.

38 Geno DiPol's Bo Huff–built 1949 Mercury four-door is one of the best looking four-door Mercs ever. Besides the radical four-inch chop, the 1954 Pontiac bumpers with accessory "wings," and the chromed 1951 Ford F1 grille with extra teeth, the car also has rounded hood corners and louvers. The spotlights are real Appletons, and the wheel covers are from a 1956 Oldsmobile.

39 DiPol's Mercury retains the factory side trim and the 1949 three-piece rear window, which some builders trade for a one-piece 1950 window or a larger 1951 window. The custom taillights are set into 1954 Pontiac accessory bumper "wings." The car is painted flat ivory with gloss ivory flames pinstriped in gold.

40 Mercury convertibles make great customs, as this modernized gold version shows. The flattened fender tips hold late model Cadillac taillights. All chrome is gone except the bumpers. The wheelwells are opened up to show off the 1957 Cadillac wheel covers.

41 Oz Kustoms in Oroville, California, is one of the premier custom builders these days. Here's an example of why the shop is held in such high regard. *Bad Apple* is as smooth as they come with flawless bodywork and paint. It's a car that traditionalists and modernists can both agree on.

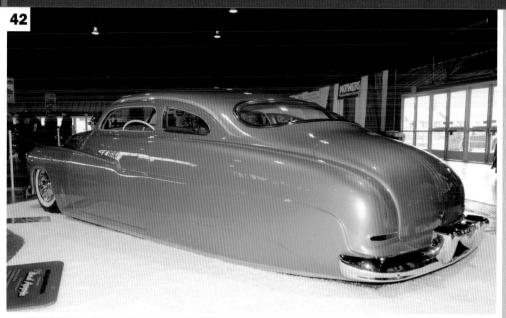

42 The Candy Apple Green paint, the scallop-style highlights, and the chrome all work together to make the Merc flow perfectly. Custom-molded taillights are similar in contour to the original equipment ones but smoother. Note the lighter-colored highlight running along the bottom of the rocker panel and into the front wheel arches.

43 An East Coast car, this Mercury displays the larger 1951 rear window. Chrome trim has been applied to the slanted B-pillar. The car sits high for a custom, at least in this photo. The taillights are from a Senior Series 1956 Packard. Note the addition of a rear quarter scoop starting at the front door beltline dip.

44 This suede green 1950 Mercury four-door is of the "drive-them-while-you-build-them" school of customs. The car is a daily driver and has the scars to prove it. It's well proportioned and could be more highly finished someday . . . or not. The owner isn't inclined to take it off the road long enough.

45 Very few Mercury four-doors have been given the "hardtop" treatment (the B-pillar removed) because the cars have suicide rear doors (the doors are hinged at the back). Here's a two-tone suede example of why more of them should be done that way. The car looks much more airy and modern with the center pillar gone.

46 It's hard to beat 1951 to 1952 DeSoto grille teeth, as this gold Merc demonstrates. Note the scoops on the side of the hood and billet wheels resembling mid-1950s Cadillac wheel covers.

47 The rear quarters and the rear bumper are from a 1951 Mercury, but the rear window is a 1950. Taillights are smoothly molded into the rear fender tips but have chrome bezels for a traditional touch.

Chapter 3
1950s Cars

Though the 1949 to 1951 Mercs and Fords might seem to be most popular among customizers, Chevrolets from the same period are very close in popularity to those FoMoCo products. Recently, the Chevy models from 1949 to 1954 have really come on strong with customizers, and they make great looking customs. More Chevys were produced in those years than Fords or Mercs too. Aftermarket parts for the Chevys also are very plentiful, and Chevy offers the advantage of parts interchangeability for its inline six-cylinder engines spanning decades of cars and trucks.

Additionally, many other brands of cars from that era make great customs. The downside to choosing a car that has been customized by many builders is that most everything that can be done has *already been* done. It'll be more difficult to come up with a unique car. On the other hand, a Pontiac or Packard or Studebaker or Dodge will attract more attention than another "same ol', same ol'." Aftermarket parts are not nearly as plentiful for these cars, but if you're building a custom car anyway, "custom" is the key word. Adapt parts as needed and create where you can.

Cars from the 1950s are modern enough that they can be very dependable drivers, even daily transportation if the owner so desires. However, they have a classic look that no modern car can ever match.

1 Brad Masterson's 1951 Chevy Fleetline sedan is a study in traditional mild customization. The top was chopped in the front, and the entire rear section, including the trunk, was dropped the same amount. Such a chop retains the smooth flow of the original top's design for a streamlined effect.

2 This 1950 Chevy Fleetline (fastback style), owned by Yenry Herrera, sits with a nose-up, taildragger style. It, too, is chopped, and its long, low look has been further enhanced by the lengthened rear fenders that incorporate upside-down 1956 Packard taillights. The grille is a 1954 Chevy center in a molded 1953 shell.

3 Originally built by Bill Cushenbery, the *Limelighter* 1958 Chevy was typical Cushenbery: tasteful but radical. The car was originally not chopped, but when current owner Bud Millard found it and restored it, he had the top chopped. One of the key themes on the car was the removal of the overload of factory chrome.

4 Dick "Peep" Jackson built the *Lil' Bastard* 1957 Ford Thunderbird when he worked for the Barris brothers in the late 1950s. The T-Bird featured emblem removal, tasteful scallops, sidepipes, and custom taillights—typical custom tricks of the day and beautifully executed.

5 Though most people today seem to want pillarless two-door hardtops, two-door sedans were also popular custom car fodder back in the 1950s. This mild 1956 Chevy sports a narrowed Lincoln front bumper, gold and white scallop paint, and a slightly lowered suspension. This is typical of a California-style daily driven custom of the late 1950s.

6

7

8

6 Bo Huff built this replica of a Barris-built 1955 Chevy convertible. The original was bought off a used car lot by Bo's friend, Stan Robles, but was ultimately destroyed. This replica is a near-perfect copy. Note the scalloped sides and the hooded rear taillights, which mimic the hooded headlights.

7 Australian Paul Zanetti created this exceptional roadster from a 1953 Cadillac Coupe de Ville. No panel on the car was left untouched. Parts of the front end and hood are from a 1952 Cadillac and were modified to smoothly flow with the 1953's subtle differences.

8 Gary Howard built this mild custom 1954 Ford Victoria in his Austin, Texas, shop for musician and custom car aficionado Jimmie Vaughan. Its subtle silver-over-white paint job belies its flawless bodywork. Howard and Vaughan have collaborated on several different beautiful customs.

9 Mark Morton's 1954 Mercury Monterey, shown here at its Grand National Roadster Show debut in 2008, is a modern-day recreation of how such a car would have been built in the 1950s. The top was chopped three inches, and the door handles and emblems were removed. Headlights and hood scoop were Frenched, and the car is lowered. Wheel covers are from a Cadillac.

10 Most people don't realize that Ford outsold Chevrolet in 1957. One look at this Bo Huff–built Fairlane 500 and there's little wonder why the Fords were so popular. Bullets-on-flat-plastic taillight lenses and four-bar Lancer wheel covers were popular accessories, as were capped single outlet (not triple) sidepipes. No chop needed; the greenhouse was perfect.

11 Hudsons from 1949 to 1952 make wonderful customs. To some folks, they already resemble a 1949 to 1951 customized Mercury. If anything, the Hudson's stock lines are smoother and less bulbous. This sedan flows even better with its chopped top and laid-down back window. Note the wraparound grille that has been extended into the wheelwells like "speed lines."

12

12 Jeff Myers built this 1956 Chevy sedan for Wichita tattoo artist Dennis McPhail, though he has since sold the car. It features a custom, handmade grille and lots of other subtle touches. The interior is by Fat Lucky's in Austin, Texas. The wheels are simple steel with inner trim rings and spiders.

13 Here's a rare 1954 Mercury, the Plexiglas-topped *Sun Valley*. On this one, the hood scoop has been removed, and the rear fender pontoons have been extended forward into the doors. The sidepipes on this one are functional and run open. Frenched headlights, very minimal paint scallops, and pink pearl paint are features.

14 Frank Livingston's Chevy Fleetline is well known in custom car circles. Its trademark 1955 Plymouth grille in a molded shell, gold paint, and white scallops are instant identifiers. The interior is white tuck and rolled. Wide whitewalls run on chrome reverse wheels.

13

14

15 Buicks like this 1956 are very popular with people looking to build a mild 1950s custom. Similar lines on 1955 to 1957 models are very clean. The rear wheel wells are radiused in stock form and look great with wire wheels like on this car. This one's been nosed and decked, and it has Frenched taillights.

16 Early 1950s Chevy Bel Air two-door hardtops make great customs, and aftermarket parts are fairly plentiful, especially mechanical ones. While this one sports a V-8 with an unusual (but period-correct) high-mounted fender-hugging exhaust, many others run original six-cylinder engines or similar, later ones.

17 Where do we start on describing this 1953 Chevy coupe by Gary "Chopit" Fioto? The top is chopped, B-pillars leaned forward, and backlight laid down. Extended rear fenders hold Packard taillights. Custom bubble fender skirts hug the body lines so tightly that they're almost invisible. The car utilizes Air Ride suspension to get so low.

18

19

20

18 This is the *Aztec* 1955 Chevy built in Barris' shop. The car is now owned by Barry Mazza. Virtually every portion of the car has been customized.

19 Kim Mejia's 1955 Lincoln Capri was built by Aiello Customs. The smooth, pink beauty is a good example of how to handle customization of an already beautiful car: tread lightly. Notice the peaked fenders, which match the peaked hood. A custom grille and removal of extraneous factory chrome doodads helped transform the car.

20 Colorado customizer Roger Jetter went the antichrome route on his chopped 1957 Chevy. A 1954 Chevy grille with extra teeth sits inside a molded and extended grille shell. The rear wheelwells mimic the shape of the fronts. Flared rocker panels continue the theme of the front pan under the grille shell. Note the scallop below the rear quarter window that breaks up the otherwise flat side.

21 It's a Kaiser, in case you were wondering. Mid-1950s Kaisers were among the most stylish of all cars, looking much like customs as built by the factory. This coupe has been treated to a top chop, lengthened rear fenders, suede paint, and a tail-dragging stance.

22 Custom car aficionado Jack Walker always liked the Barris Brothers' 1951 Buick, built for Lyle Lake of Florida. The original no longer exists, so Walker commissioned a clone of the car, built by Kenny Baker of Missouri and Dick Huckins of Oklahoma. The top is chopped three inches in front and twice that in the rear.

23 Changing to a smaller rear window and considerably widening the C-pillars on this Cadillac as the top was being chopped significantly altered the appearance, giving it a profile similar to a Carson top.

24 Here's an unusual adaptation: a 1957 Mercury two-door station wagon. The Mercury's distinctive front end has given way to a more nondescript treatment with a full-width bar grille, 1957 Chevy headlights and fender sections, and a single-level 1959 Plymouth bumper. The top was chopped 2.5 inches and rear side windows were filled.

25 Here's a different take on a station wagon: a 1955 Chevy two-door. A Corvette grille with extra teeth, radiused rear wheel wells, and chopped top are the first things to catch the eye. The car is matte black with a purple metalflake roof, Frenched headlights, and modified 1955 Pontiac side trim.

26 The first of the Wide Track Pontiacs, this 1959 Bonneville hardtop is clean and classy. Stock side trim remains; it's a popular addition to other customs. The mild custom treatment to this car consists mostly of door handle and chrome trim removal, wire wheels with knock-offs, and a custom interior and paint.

27 A work in progress, this California 1954 Mercury two-door sedan is being enjoyed by its owner as he works on it. The top has been chopped, B-pillars slanted, and rear window and C-pillar areas revised with a smaller window and wider pillars. Some builders do that to avoid having to cut the wraparound rear window; others do it because they like the more formal look.

28 Richard Zocchi commissioned Gene Winfield to build this 1958 Chrysler, *Golden Sunrise*. John D'Agostino later owned it. Art Himsl painted the car, which is chopped and has extended fenders and 1972 Oldsmobile headlights.

29 This Chevy carries all of the traditional customizer's touches: molded grille shell with simple single bar grille, molded gravel pans (between bumper and body), shaved door handles, Cadillac wheel covers, chopped top, dual spotlights, and lowered stance. It's also nosed and decked (chrome trim removed from hood and trunk) and slightly lower in the rear.

30

31

32

30 Rear fenders extended seven inches to adapt 1955 DeSoto taillights and a 1958 Studebaker bumper give this chopped 1953 Chevy a completely different look. The chop involved whacking four inches out of the front and six inches out of the rear and then smoothing everything proportionally.

31 "Voodoo" Larry Grobe's trademark 1953 Chevy is almost unrecognizable as such. It's named *Voodoo Kreeper*. Literally every piece has been altered. It's radically chopped and has a tilt front end. Note the sculpted side panels, custom bubble fender skirts, Dagmar bumper, and Packard taillights.

32 Eryk Frias' 1953 Oldsmobile was an old custom from the 1960s, and all of its major body mods were done in lead and with perfect nosed, decked, shaved, and Frenched elements. He found the car on eBay and had Donnie Baird at Imperial Customs do the scalloped paint job.

33 Oldsmobile called its fastbacks like this 1950 version "Club Sedans," and like their Chevy and Pontiac corporate sisters, they make great customs. They respond well to shaving of extraneous trim and door handles, a mild lowering, and some subtle custom touches.

34 Look closely. This 1956 Mercury has been chopped and sectioned, but the front end remains at stock height. The treatment radically alters the appearance of the car, which retains the majority of its chrome and stainless stock trim, other than emblems.

35 Check out the difference between the chopped 1954 Plymouth in the foreground and the stock height roof on the one behind it. New Jersey's Mark Wojcik of Customs by Flash has also lowered the car and Frenched the headlights.

36 Here's another good example of a custom mid-1950s Buick, this one with a 1956 Oldsmobile front bumper and a Corvette grille. Tunneled vertical quad headlights, a louvered hood, and miles-deep scalloped paint finish off the treatment.

37 This East Coast 1954 Mercury has been around for a long time. Built originally by John Pazsik around 1959, it was recently redone. It has scalloped front fenders, extended and scooped rear quarters, an extended and Frenched hood scoop, and a molded rear bumper, among other touches.

38 Tattoo artist Baby Ray didn't have to do a whole lot to make his 1951 Packard distinctive. Packards start out that way. This one is shaved, lowered, and smoothed out. It has a removable Carson-style top and that big chrome Packard grille, which he wisely did not change.

39 Dustin Cooper's 1955 DeSoto is a 1950s-style, drive-as-you-build car. The top has been chopped; the taillights are from a 1956 Packard. The top was stripped to bare metal, polished, and sprayed with clear. The car runs a stock Hemi. It has been driven cross country and run at the Newport (Indiana) Hill Climb.

40 How about a custom for families? This 1959 Ford Galaxie four-door sedan has a front bumper and grille from a 1957 DeSoto, cruiser fender skirts, and a cool scalloped paint job. Note the two-level eyebrows over the headlights. The cone wheel covers are from a 1957 Plymouth.

41 Proof that a custom doesn't need to be radical to be outstanding, this purple and lavender 1958 Ford Fairlane 500 retains its identity but with a transformed personality. The rear fins have been raised and extended, and the front grille shell is molded and holds a 1959 Imperial grille. The headlights were moved back into extended fenders.

39

40

41

42

42 George Kilger's 1951 Chevy coupe was customized in the late 1950s and was in several magazines back then. The golden beauty has a 1955 DeSoto grille in a custom shell, 1955 Chevy headlight "eyebrows," and a handmade nerf bar where the bumper used to live.

43 Rocker James Hetfield and customizer Rick Dore collaborated on Hetfield's 1953 Buick Skylark. It has a removable Carson-style top, angled custom side windows, and scoops on the hood sides. Trademark Buick headlights, the kind often appropriated for other customs, reside in custom housings.

43

44 Here's a low 1951 Chevy coupe with an attitude. The grille is a 1953 Chevy piece with extra added where the parking lights would have been. The headlights look to be from a 1955 Oldsmobile. The door vent windows have been removed, and the top is chopped.

44

45 Relatively stock, this primered 1955 Pontiac four-door sedan has been lowered, shaved, and decked. The hood has been removed too. It even has stock Pontiac wheel covers, which most people wouldn't recognize as anything but custom anyway. It has Mexican blankets for seat covers and a furry rug in the pack package shelf. Side pipes complete the "hot rod custom" look.

46 You've heard "Anyone can restore a car, but it takes a real man to cut one up," right? Rick Dore must be a real man because he cut the top off a 1957 Lincoln Continental Mark II to build this custom.

47 1955 Plymouths often lend their parts to other customs. The grille is an especially stylish and tasteful item. This Plymouth was made into a mild custom, using lowering, nosing, and decking as main tools. It has 1955 Pontiac side trim and bubble fender skirts.

45

46

47

Chapter 4
1960s Cars

You may notice that there aren't as many cars in this section as in previous ones. That's because there aren't as many custom 1960s cars as there are from the 1940s and 1950s. Why? It's probably because by the 1960s, American cars were almost customs as they came from the factory. There were dozens of different colors, different trim levels—at least three or four per car brand—plus different rooflines, various interior colors, and seating arrangements—bucket and bench seats. The stylists at the major manufacturers were doing the customizers' jobs for them. With new cars like the 1963 to 1965 Buick Riviera, Ford Thunderbird, Pontiac Grand Prix, and Oldsmobile Starfire available—and financeable—there was less compulsion to customize.

Still, 1960s cars do respond to customizing, but the builder must be careful not to mess up an already good design. For those with questionable taste, customizing a 1960s car can be an exercise in futility. It's not unlike the mistakes made with current "tuner cars," where an owner will bolt or glue on all the latest aftermarket wings and fender flares and spoilers and faux carbon fiber and plastic "chrome" and wind up with a clown car.

The concept of "customizing with paint," introduced by Larry Watson on his 1958 Thunderbird (see chapter 10), is alive and well in the world of 1960s customs. There are few radical 1960s customs but plenty of pretty ones.

1 One of the iconic 1960s customs is the Alexander Brothers' 1960 Pontiac, *Golden Indian*. It is so tastefully done (as were all A-Brothers cars) that it should be the subject of a textbook on customs. The front and rear were completely reworked using tube grilles and lights with plastic fins. The inset side molding was retained. The wheels are simple chrome reversed with two-bar spinner caps.

2 *Thunderflite* is Dean Arnold's 1961 Ford Thunderbird. The car has a bubble top, exaggerated upper and lower fins, a rocker panel–skirted exhaust, and an Air Ride suspension. It's one of the most radical 1960s customs to come along in awhile.

3 Mild customization works great on 1960s cars like this 1964 Ford Galaxie. Removal of most all chrome trim, except the bumpers and grille, lets the sculpted sides shine. The silver body and red metalflake roof are a good combination, and the stance and wheels are just right. This is a statement of good taste.

4 Here's another 1960 Pontiac, the same model that the *Golden Indian* started as. This one retains the stock grille but adds a 1950s Indian head hood ornament and two-tone paint with graphics and scallops.

5 Here's John D'Agostino's 1961 Oldsmobile hardtop. It features a barely discernable fadeaway paint job, a 1960 Mercury grille, and wire wheels. Like all of D'Agostino's cars, this one is tasteful, subtle, and extremely well crafted.

6 Richard Zocchi took a completely different approach to his 1961 Oldsmobile than D'Agostino. Zocchi cut off the Olds bubble top and grafted on a Ford Starliner roof, chopping it in the process and widening the C-pillars and using a Camaro rear window. Custom fender skirts follow the line of the rocker panels and incorporate the rear finned flare as well.

7 Another D'Agostino car, this 1966 Oldsmobile follows the paint customization track. The car has been nosed, decked, and shaved, and then it got a Winfield-style fadeaway paint job and a subtle custom grille.

8 Kevin Anderson's *Gold Top* 1963 Buick Riviera was built by John Kouw of Cruisin' Customs. Besides the custom mix gold paint, it features a 2.5-inch chop, tube grille, and 1967 Imperial headlights. The Riviera's stock hood peak was also removed.

9 This East Coast 1965 Riviera has also been chopped, shaved, nosed, and decked. It features wire wheels that follow the custom theme, but the ground effects are an unusual choice for a personal luxury car, especially a custom.

10 Richie Cordova's *Colorado Springs* 1960 Cadillac is striking. A 1960 Caddy already looks like a tastefully customized 1959 Cadillac, so it doesn't require much work. Mostly this one received a shave and lowering and some great paint work.

11 Other than the wheels, this is a beautiful car, a 1965 Pontiac Bonneville. The wheels do not fit the style of the car. Like most customs, cars from the 1960s look best with components no more than maybe five years newer than the car. Trying to leap 40-plus years with a set of wheels doesn't work.

12 and 13 Built by Gambino Kustoms for *Goodguys Gazette* editor Kirk Jones, this 1960 Ford Starliner is one of the coolest 1960s-style customs to come along in a long, long time. It won shows everywhere it went, and it's easy to see why. From one end to the other, it's a knockout, starting at the custom grille and running along the paneled and laced paint to the custom-made Bellflower exhaust pipes, the nylon and vinyl interior . . . and you name it.

14 Bo Huff's *Tamale Leaf* 1962 Thunderbird is a custom-by-paint car if there ever was one. It features metalflake, flames, ground glass, cobwebbing, and scallops. Beyond that, it's been nosed and decked and has Bellflower exhaust pipes behind the back wheels and lakes dumps behind the front wheels.

15 Gary Howard from Austin, Texas, is one of the most respected custom builders working today. He has built several cars for blues singer/guitarist Jimmie Vaughan. This 1960 Chevy Impala was built for Mike Young. Chopped slightly over an inch, the car was flamed and scalloped by Rod Powell. Its abalone pearl paint, applied by Howard, is flawless.

16 It took some real custom vision to even imagine this modification, a Ford Starliner roof on a Thunderbird. It works, though. That's the kind of thinking that separates the men from the boys in the custom world!

17 The author's 1964 Buick Riviera *Car Kulture DeLuxe* project car is under construction at Masterson Kustoms of L.A. Brad Masterson chopped the top, laid out by Bill Hines, 5 1/2 inches and laid the back section of the top forward, keeping the rear window intact. The wire wheels are by Truespoke. The car will get extended fenders and a few other special touches.

18 Here's one of those cars you can't mess with much without screwing it up: a 1962 Pontiac Grand Prix. This one's just fine, though, showing a slightly chopped top, molded-in sidepipes, and tasteful removal of what little bit of chrome trim (and door handles) came on the car. Those wheels are factory option, eight-lug aluminum finned wheels from 1962; too cool to replace.

19 Pontiacs from the 1960s make great customs because they were already General Motors' most stylish cars. This 1966 Bonneville has been lowered, nosed, decked, and shaved. Chrome bullets adorn the grille, and Moon Sunburst wheel covers have a bullet in the center too. The ribbed trim on the lower sides was stock and serves to help make the already long and low car look even more so.

20 and 21 This is the author's 1961 Pontiac Ventura, customized by Bo Huff, and painted by Bo and Junior Huff. The car has had the door handles and most chrome trim removed, except the wind splits on the tops of the fenders. Chrome was added to the front grille surrounds, the cowl vent panel, and the pan between the bumper and grilles. Molded sidepipes also were added. The taillights are from a 1961 Buick.

22 *Galaxy* is a 1967 Buick Riviera styled by Darryl Starbird and the car's owner Jim Unrein. Starbird did the bubble top and front end in 1976. Unrein did the rest in 1975. The car is on loan to Darryl Starbird's Hall of Fame Museum near Afton, Oklahoma.

23 Alex and Suzie Gambino of Gambino Kustoms own this 1964 Pontiac, which they drive everywhere. It features a low stance, a drawer-pull grille, and suede pearl paint with scallops. Sidepipes and chrome reverse wheels with Shannon cones top it off.

24 John D'Agostino's 1961 Olds Starfire convertible was a joint effort between Bill Hines and Oz Customs. Bill chopped the windshield and convertible top, did the sunken antennas, and installed the 1959 Imperial grille.

25 Not a common subject for a custom, and not a commonly seen car in stock form, Mark Wojcik's 1961 Dodge makes a striking one. The car was started by a friend, and Mark acquired it from another friend in a trade. It's well known all over the New Jersey and Northeast custom car scene.

26 Like the 1960 Cadillac is to the 1959 Caddy, the 1960 Buick looks like a tastefully customized version of the over-the-top 1959 Buick. The 1960s surfaces and edges were smoothed. They don't require much work other than lowering and adding a little nice paint and some cool wheels.

27 Richard Zocchi's baby blue 1964 Pontiac Grand Prix is a classic. The top is chopped, chrome trim removed, front fenders extended, and outboard backup lights Frenched. Wire wheels finish off the classy cruiser.

28 Here's a mid-1960s Dodge Dart that has undergone the custom treatment, spotted at the Yokohama, Japan, Mooneyes show. The car has been radically chopped and received a Carson-style top. A bullet-laden grille sits between green-lensed "space alien" headlights.

29 Californian Gary Minor created a "phantom" 1962 Pontiac Grand Prix wagon by combining a four-door Catalina wagon and a Grand Prix coupe. It required more work than you might think as he used the longer doors from the two-door Grand Prix, so he had to fabricate new door jambs, among other things.

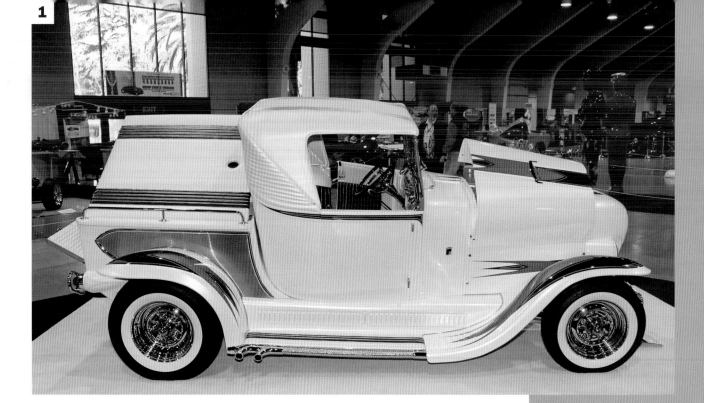

Chapter 5
Show Rods, Trucks, & Late Models

Almost any car can be made into a custom, although some cars lend themselves more readily to the customizer's hand than others. The key to choosing a custom car project is to pick a car you like.

Generally, cars from about 1936 through the mid-1960s are considered the best ones to customize, but there have been some from before and after that 30-odd year range that work. Cars like the Richard Peters/Barris Kustoms 1929 Ford, *Ala Kart,* and Bill Hines' 1934 *Golden Nugget* are famous "show rods" or "custom rods" created from pre-1936 cars. There have also been a few post mid-1960s ones, but none have really gained notoriety or even much acceptance

among custom-car aficionados. Customizer Bill Hines is a huge fan of those and has built a few. He drives one daily.

Some builders have chosen to build one-off customs, utilizing either a production chassis or one they've created themselves. To that they've added complete custom bodies made of steel, aluminum, or fiberglass. The result is usually a car with an appearance that belies its origins. Some are strikingly beautiful.

In any case, a custom is an individual's car. As such, it should reflect the tastes of its owner. Here are a few examples of cars that do just that. They don't fit into our other chapter categories of customs, but they are customs nonetheless.

1 Without a doubt, the most famous show rod of all time is the Barris-built *Ala Kart.* Built from a Ford Model A pickup for (and with the assistance of) owner Richard Peters, the *Ala Kart* won the World's Most Beautiful Roadster Award at the Grand National Roadster Show in 1958. It won again in 1959.

2 Restored even beyond its original glory by Roy Brizio, the *Ala Kart* was again entered at the Grand National Roadster Show in 2008, 50 years after first winning there. The car is now owned by John Mumford.

3 Ed "Big Daddy" Roth built some of the best-known show rods of the 1960s, and most were turned into model kits by Revell. Customizer and painter Fritz "Spritz by Fritz" Schenk reverse engineered and built this clone of Roth's *Outlaw* using a Revell kit as his pattern.

4 The *Car Craft Dream Rod* was another famous show rod. Built in 1963 by Bill Cushenbery, it was an exceptionally sporty and modern-looking car for its time. Mark Moriarity now owns the car and has recently restored it. It rides on Ford Thunderbird Kelsey-Hayes wire wheels.

5 One of the outstanding features of the *Dream Rod* is its asymmetrical design. AMT model company produced a model kit of the car in 1963, and it was very popular among young custom car fans. If one can be found, the kits bring relatively big money from collectors today.

6 *Golden Nugget* is a 1934 Ford roadster built by world-famous customizer Bill Hines. It was a class winner at Detroit Autorama in 1958. It was restored by its current owner, Jackson, Michigan, custom car builder Larry Jordon, and won the Preservation Award at Detroit in 2005.

7 Elden Titus built the one-off, bubble-top *Vampyre* for Gary Meyers. A regular show winner everywhere it appeared, *Vampyre* was a full-size rendition of a scratch-built model car that Titus built as a youngster.

8 The *Vibrasonic Roadster* is another Elden Titus creation, one he was working on when he passed away in late 2008. Fellow custom builders and friends have vowed to finish the car, which was being built in collaboration with George Barris and *Car Kulture DeLuxe* magazine. It features a hand-formed steel body over tube framework.

9 *El Tiki* is a twenty-first century homage to the show rods of the early 1960s. Built by Tom Culbertson of Culberston's Rods & Customs in Indianapolis, it is owned by John and Susie Cooper. The 1928 Model A sport coupe body is channeled over a custom tube frame. Power is provided by a 324 Oldsmobile Rocket engine.

10 *El Tiki*'s front end is a collaboration by original builder Culbertson and owner Cooper, along with Cooper's son, Dustin. The mostly hand-formed grille shell utilizes grille mesh from a 1958 Ford and 40 chrome-plated drawer pulls. The headlight pods are a combination of highly modified 1960 Buick front fender pieces backed by 1936 Dodge headlight buckets.

Custom Trucks

11 Customizers had cool shop trucks back in the early days. The Barris shop's *Kopper Kart* Chevy pickup was no exception. The original is long gone, but Vic Collins (owner), John Maurice, and Mark Wojcik have built a beautiful replica of the truck at Wojcik's New Jersey shop, Customs by Flash.

12 Though certainly not a clone of the *Kopper Kart*, this California Chevy was obviously inspired by it. Its simpler rear end treatment still flows well. It would be possible to retain a working tailgate on a truck similar to this, allowing a greater level of utility.

13 The *Rod & Custom Dream Truck* was the brainchild of that magazine's first editor, Spencer Murray. Documented in numerous tech articles in the magazine, beginning in late 1953, the truck passed through several iconic customizers' shops, including those of Gene Winfield, the Barris brothers, Bob Metz, and Valley Custom.

14 Dave Pareso, owner of Back Street Kustoms in Colorado Springs, didn't build this truck, but it has become one of his trademark vehicles anyway and serves as his shop truck. The rear fins incorporate 1960 Chrysler taillights. The front and rear fenders are molded in, and the truck runs Radir wheels.

15 Here's an example of a clean, mild custom pickup. One like this—lightly chopped, slightly lowered, but still at a daily-drivable height—could be used as dependable transportation with lots of style. Aftermarket replacement parts abound for these trucks, making them eminently usable vintage customs.

16 Other than lowering, the large sun visor, and the nice late 1960s wheels (Indy 500 Drag Mags), this circa 1953 Chevy truck is mostly stock. It was photographed by *Car Kulture DeLuxe* feature editor Anna Marco at the Mooneyes car show in Yokohama, Japan.

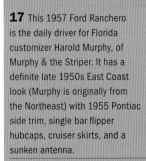

17 This 1957 Ford Ranchero is the daily driver for Florida customizer Harold Murphy, of Murphy & the Striper. It has a definite late 1950s East Coast look (Murphy is originally from the Northeast) with 1955 Pontiac side trim, single bar flipper hubcaps, cruiser skirts, and a sunken antenna.

18 Still (or maybe always to be) in primer, this Chevy pickup has a lot of cool touches, including a chopped top and full fender skirts. Custom pods house 1959 Cadillac taillights. Notice that the exhaust runs through the bed rails, which are capped off with tractor-style flappers.

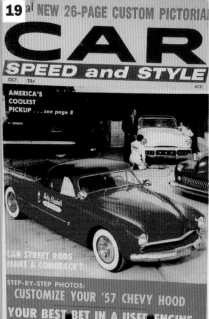

19 through 21 Featured in the October 1958 issue of *Car Speed and Style* magazine was this 1949 Ford convertible-turned-pickup. With a sectioned body and lift-off roof, it was the Betty Elizabeth Shampoo company's truck back then. It's now owned by Doug Silva, who has plans to restore it.

22 Gene Winfield's shop truck and rolling business card in the 1950s was this 1935 Ford. Typical for Winfield, the truck was very tastefully done. It has custom front split bumpers with molded gravel pans and mesh inserts, molded sidepipes, a custom bar grille, a chopped top, and a louvered hood.

23

23 Look up "stylish pickup" in any dictionary and a 1959 Chevy El Camino will be in there. This one is simple and smooth with Astro Supreme wheels, Air Ride lowering, and the emblems and door panels removed. The main body is painted metallic green while the roof and inside the bed are metalflake.

24 Gary Meyers' 1959 El Camino got the full custom treatment. The tailgate was welded closed, and a full molded bed cover was added. The familiar 1959 Chevy cat's eye taillights have been replaced with reshaped custom housings and lenses. The custom rolled rear pan is capped by a narrow, split, and molded bumper.

25 The Chevelle-based El Caminos, such as this 1964 model, make great customs too. This one is lowered and has chrome reverse wheels. The door handles and emblems were removed, and the car got a nice 1960s-style scallop paint job. Note the Bellflower-style exhaust pipes behind the rear wheels.

24

25

26 Gene Winfield built this Chevy truck for a Japanese customer. It has a pie-cut and sectioned hood, molded fender skirts, and a chopped top. Gene made a custom bar grille for the truck and painted it in one of his trademark fadeaway paint jobs. Below the grille is a custom flared rolled pan.

27 A favorite among restorers, as well as customizers, is the 1956 Ford pickup. This one has a 1962 Chrysler grille filled with chrome drawer pull knobs, flanked by the canted Chrysler headlights. A top chop, emblem and door handle removal, single Buick portholes in the hood, and added short sidepipes complete the custom work. The paint is matte pearl blue.

28 Here's another take on a Ford pickup, though a 1954 or 1955 model (angled A-pillar as opposed to the 1956 vertical one). This one's chopped, and the vent windows have been removed. It also has the Chrysler grille treatment, which is popular for these trucks. The grille is filled with Pontiac fender stars, though.

29

30

31

29 Lots of work has been done to this Ford pickup. It's chopped and slammed and has full fender skirts with scoops added. The bed rails received a set of finned additions molded in, as is the rear bumper with bullets. Molded sidepipes extend past the fronts of the rear wheelwells.

30 No, Ford did not make a Ranchero in 1955. This one is converted from a car and is very nicely done. The top was chopped during the process, and a molded grille shell holds a horizontal bar grille. Above it are Frenched headlights; below is a molded pan.

31 The rear window and roof appear to be from a 1957 to 1958 Ranchero. The door handles were removed, as were emblems, though the stylish 1955 side trim remains. The taillights are Frenched 1956 Mercury station wagon lights. The rear rolled pan matches the front.

32 This chopped early 1950s Chevy pickup is now wearing a Cadillac grille and a narrowed Cadillac bumper. The solid rear fenders are likely removable from inside the bed to facilitate rear wheel removal and maintenance. The headlights are Frenched, and the running boards have been removed.

One-Off Customs

33 This car is titled as a 1957 DeSoto, and that's where its drivetrain and dashboard came from. The rest of it is pure custom, but many of its sheetmetal parts seem to have started life on a 1950 Dodge, although they're highly modified. The original builder of the car is unknown. Some features, such as the 1953 Buick headlights, are unquestioned.

34 The car is sectioned as compared to a normal production car's body height, which necessitates a fairly tall greenhouse in proportion. The taillights are 1950 Dodge units, a very clean design for adaptation into cars of that period. The bumpers and front wheelwells seem to give credence to the 1950 Dodge body donor car theory.

35

36

37

35 The *Skylane Motor Special* was built between 1948 and 1951. It has a full custom metal body on a 1932 Ford chassis. The grille is from a 1948 Cadillac, and the car has Lincoln Continental rear fenders and Mercury bumpers. It was featured in *Motor Trend*, the June 1951 issue, and *Car Kulture DeLuxe* issue No. 19.

36 Give up? It's a Buick Riviera, 1988 to 1989 style. Long Beach, California, customizer Bill Hines is a fan of the cars and has built a couple into customs including this one, which he sometimes drives daily. He calls it *Lil' Bat*, and it sports his trademark fins and custom-formed cat's eye-shaped taillight housings.

37 Bill Hines' personal Cadillac Seville is another example of his affinity for the mid-1980s GM front-drive luxury cars. His finned C-pillar sail panels and extended front fenders accentuate the Seville's already distinguished profile. He's also added twin molded-in sidepipes and removed door handles and all extraneous trim.

38 Named *41 Bat*, Bill Hines' 1983 Riviera was customized by him in 1985. It is on permanent loan to Darryl Starbird's Rod & Custom Hall of Fame Museum in Oklahoma. This car got a full frontal treatment with a new custom grille and reshaped fenders. The bumpers are rear bumpers from a 1960s Corvette Sting Ray.

39 This end is what inspired *41 Bat*'s name. The custom rear sheetmetal and rear window are reminiscent of a 1941 Buick's, though the fins certainly are not. The rear bumpers are Corvette items like the front, joined by an overrider.

40 Properly applied, customizing techniques work on any car. This is a Mitsubishi Debonair sedan, probably from the early 1970s. It has the classic lowered stance, custom bar grille, shaved emblems and door handles, fender skirts, and custom cone wheel covers. The paint is candy copper with traditional pinstriping.

Chapter 6
Style & Flow

The coolness and flow of a custom car go from front to rear. Most observers will see the front first, whether walking through a parking lot full of cars or watching the car coming down the road toward them. The car's overall appearance flows like a rocket or an airplane, the front beginning the impression, which then follows smoothly along the fuselage/body and ends with the tail or rear end.

In creating a custom car, the builder is taking another person's creation, the car designed by a professional designer, and attempting to improve upon it. It had better be good! Ideally, a custom car's design should flow so well that it looks like it *could* have been built by the factory.

And though the car is viewed as an overall work, it is accomplished in small sections. That makes it doubly important for the builder to have an overall plan so that he doesn't get distracted or lose course somewhere. We've probably all seen customs where it is obvious the builder either didn't have a plan or he had exceptionally bad taste. Such cars look like the builder picked a few single elements that he liked but gave no thought as to how they worked together. The final result is a car that is uglier than the original and an insult to the original car's designer.

Here are some ideas for design elements that work well from beautiful cars that had smooth, cohesive designs.

1 John D'Agostino is the master of beautiful cars that look like the factory built them—or should have! His 1958 Oldsmobile, *The Egyptian*, is an example. The car is chopped and smoothed but retains some of the factory chrome that made the stock version a standout. It's probably very close to what the car's original designer would have built if left to his own devices.

2 Here's another car that flows well, John Spencer's 1939 Ford convertible, built by Dave Kinnaman and modified by Gary Minor at the instruction of a previous owner. The Packard grille is a favorite among builders of this style of car as it brings the air of an upscale car to the more common Ford. The fenders are molded, headlights Frenched, and running boards removed.

3 Chopping the top is one area where a custom's style can be won or lost. This one is a beautiful chop, done in a hardtop (pillarless) style with angled front, and fixed rear windows. Note that the front vent windows have been retained, which is in keeping with this style of 1949 to 1951 Mercury custom.

4 Here's a perfect chop on a four-door 1949 Mercury, owned by Geno DiPol, built by Bo Huff Customs. The radically chopped top flows so well that even other builders love this car. The car sits low but on conventional suspension, not air bags, so it's a comfortable driver. This car has small-block Chevy power, four doors, and full working suspension. It could be used as a family car and cost less than a new Buick.

5 Here's a view to show just a few of the many ways to chop a 1949 to 1951 Mercury. All three of these cars are from that range, yet each one is drastically different from the next. Rear window shapes and how they flow into the trunk lids are different as are the side window profiles. There's no "best way" to chop a Merc.

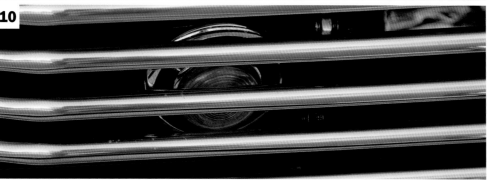

6 Here's an alternative to louvers in the hood: three flared and molded custom portholes. They serve to help release heat from under the hood, as well as to add a styling touch. See how much better and more stylish these look than the goofy plastic chrome stick-on "portholes" available at Walmart and AutoZone?

7 Not everyone likes *El Matador*, the radical custom 1940 Ford coupe built by Bill Cushenbery in the 1960s and later restored from a charred hulk by Harold Murphy, its current owner. There's no mistaking the car's style and its smooth flow, though. Cushenbery obviously maintained the same vision from one end of the car to the other.

8 through 10 The Alexander Brothers were kings among men with their beautiful customs in the 1960s. The *Golden Chariot* 1956 Chevy, owned and restored by Lou Calasibetta of Old Stillwater Garage, is one such car. From the modified side trim to the full-length sidepipes, all of the elements the A-Brothers added visually lengthen and lower the car. Even the single asymmetrical scoop on the hood is blended in low and wide, complementing the wide, full-width bar grille. Hidden behind the grille, but still large enough to be useful, are the round turn signals/parking lights.

11 The fake scoop on the roof of the author's 1961 Pontiac is from a 1959 Chevy Impala. It fits the style of the car, as the Impala had a similar roofline. The interior, which is always visible through the nearly all-glass GM bubble top, follows the early 1960s theme of the car. A newer styled interior would have looked out of place.

12 Here's another roof scoop, molded in and with chrome teeth. It's similar to the ones from 1954 Mercurys, sometimes seen on fender skirts of early 1950s cars.

13 On his 1958 Ford Thunderbird, legendary painter Larry Watson diminished the prominent hood scoop by painting it and the surrounding hood a dark color, but then accentuated it by painting the silver panel and tying it to the cowl grilling. The result visually lowers the scoop, though no metal was cut. Watson owned the concept of "customizing with paint."

14 This is a 1958 Chevy Impala with a couple of twists. Mark Wojcik removed the chrome "grille" at the end and then extended, peaked, and molded the scoop. Inside resides a third brake light.

15

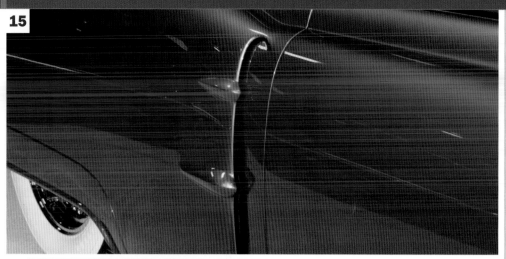

16

17

18

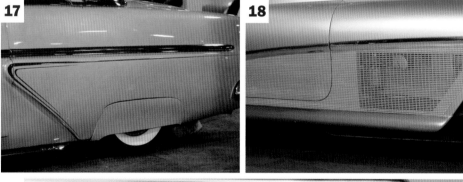

19

15 One trick that customizers use is to accentuate or embellish on the original car's features, taking them one step further (or more). Such is the side scoop on this mid-1950s Cadillac. Cadillac originally used a chromed diecast fake scoop with black painted "holes." This one has real scoops, running almost from the beltline to the rocker panels.

16 Using one piece windshields on cars that didn't have them is a familiar way to update a car when customizing it. The *El Matador*'s windshield is now not only one piece, but it's curved too.

17 Rather than use long, pointed (and heavy) fender skirts on his 1954 Mercury, this builder extended the fender "pontoons" instead, clear up into the doors. The effect is that of lengthening the fenders. The tasteful scallops accentuate the new shape without being gaudy.

18 The front fenders on GM's Harley Earl–style *LeSabre* dream car feature nearly hidden grilles, a concept that could be adapted to custom cars, allowing for air flow and brake cooling on the sides. Used in the front, headlights or turn signals could go behind such grilles; it would work in the rear for taillights.

19 Louvers have long been favorites of customizers and hot rodders. They add a traditional touch and help vent heat from under the hood too. They also let dirt and water in, though.

20 The style and flow of John Cooper's *El Tiki* show rod starts right here and flows seamlessly through the interior and to the rear of the car. There's no doubt from looking at the front end of this car what its purpose is—it's an all-out, one-of-a-kind show rod. Period.

21 Here's a novel example of some "custom thinking" on this Hudson. The grille bars wrap around and actually extend into the front edges of the wheelwells. These chrome extensions serve as "speed lines," visually lowering and lengthening the car a little bit.

22 Though much of the extra chrome trim is often removed on a custom, some pieces deserve to stay. Such is case for this cormorant hood ornament on tattoo artist Baby Ray's Packard. The elegant Packard grille, heavy on chrome, is also a welcome piece, better than most anything that could have been grafted into its place.

23 This Chevy Fleetline, styled and built by Brown's Metal Mods in Indianapolis, has wonderful flow and continuity of design. Note the similar flowing arcs of the side windows, the rear fenders, the custom-made fender skirts, and the scalloped coves in the side. The chopped top flows back into a boat tail on the rear deck, further accenting the shape. The car is like a wheeled speedboat at speed.

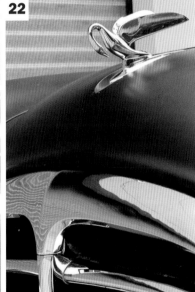

24 Overall style—that is the flow of Yenry Herrera's Chevy Fleetline. The entire car flows smoothly and nearly seamlessly to the back bumper. Even the taillights point to that, as does the sculpted swiggle extension from the rain gutters and behind the rear quarter windows.

25 Okay, use your imagination on this one. The foundation is there on this Cadillac sedan, chopped by Brad Masterson at Masterson Kustoms of L.A., to make one very cool custom; a four-door, no less. Most people look for a Cadillac two-door hardtop, so the use of a four-door is stepping outside the norm. That's what customs are about.

26 Twin sunken antennas were a popular feature in the 1960s. These are in the driver side door of the Alexander Brothers' 1960 Pontiac, *Golden Indian*. The raised rib between them is a nice touch.

27 The upper side trim is stock on Gordy Brown's 1954 Ford, but the three side spears are from a 1954 Mercury, dressing up the less flashy Ford a bit.

28 Sculpting bodylines can add some visual excitement to an otherwise slab-sided car. Witness the swooping, tapered line added to Baby Ray's Packard. These can be done with steel rod, shaped and welded to the body, and then filled with either lead or body filler.

29 Mark Wojcik's 1961 Dodge has had sculpted scoops added to the roof. The feature was then accented with Larry Watsonesque scallops.

30 The rear nerf bars on *El Matador* mimic the contour of the rear deck lid, as well as that of the rear fenders. The lines are repeated in the coves in the fenders, as well as the ribs on the deck lid.

31 Bullnose hood strips were sold by such companies as Honest Charley, J. C. Whitney, Almquist, and other parts purveyors back in the day. They were used to replace the hood ornament and factory moldings on the hood of mildly customized cars. They bolt into the stock holes but give a smoother profile.

32 and 33 Oz Welch of Oz Customs peaked the fenders and the headlight rims on John D'Agostino's 1957 Oldsmobile. They look like they came that way from the factory, which was exactly the point. The hood peak has been extended down to where the big Olds hood medallion used to be. That's one of the marks of a well-executed custom. It looks different but natural.

29

30

31

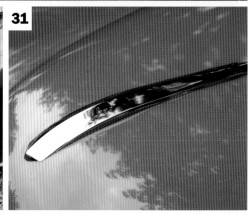

32

33

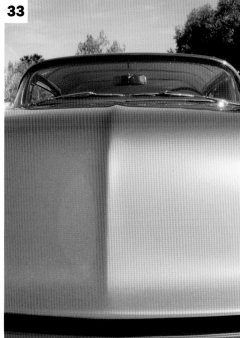

34

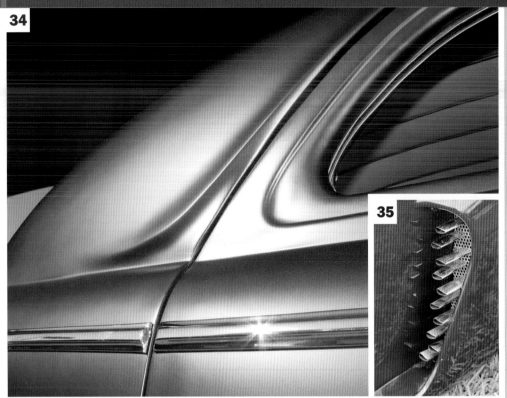

35

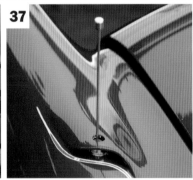

36

37

38

34 A little smoothing and sculpting accentuates the long, low, lean forward look of Ron Gomez's 1941 Buick coupe. It's little touches like these that separate a ho-hum car from one that catches the eyes of those in the know.

35 The grilles within the side rear fender scoops on *El Matador* are constructed of the same perforated metal and the identical teardrop tubing as the grille. Not only does such a treatment stand out as out of the ordinary, it also continues the theme of the front end. Style and flow emit from this car at every angle.

36 These sculpted scoops are on the sides of the hood on a 1946–1948 Chevy. They are smooth and not too obvious. They look like they belong there.

37 Here's an interesting twist of an antenna. Instead of sinking it, the builder left it surface-mounted but built a small, sculpted scoop over it and put the antenna through a hole in the scoop. Pinstriping accents the scoop.

38 Trim from similarly bodied vehicles within the same corporate family can be adapted to other cars in the same family. This 1954 Chevy is decorated with the downward peaked beltline trim from a 1953 or 1954 Pontiac. Those cars all used the same roof sections, so the trim fits. The same can be done among 1949 to 1952 Chevys, Pontiacs, and Oldsmobiles.

39 Shrouded, straight, bologna-sliced sidepipes were a popular 1960s modification for customs. The author's Bo Huff–built 1961 Pontiac Ventura has them. They help to visually lower and lengthen the car, especially when it's lowered on its Air Ride suspension below the height shown here.

40 Continuing the style of the early 1960s are the four-bar spinner wheel covers, the red-painted wheels, and the wide whitewall tires. As a concession to modernity (and better ride and handling), the tires are Coker Classic radials rather than the more correct bias-ply tires of the era. Reproduction bias ply tires from the original molds are available, though.

41 The front end of this Chevy starts a smooth and simple style that carries through the rest of the car. Traditional customs, or at least the best of them, were tasteful and simple, not garish. This one follows that preferred theme.

42

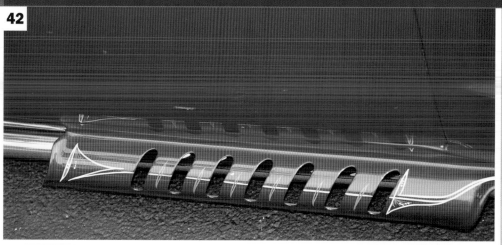

43

44

45

46

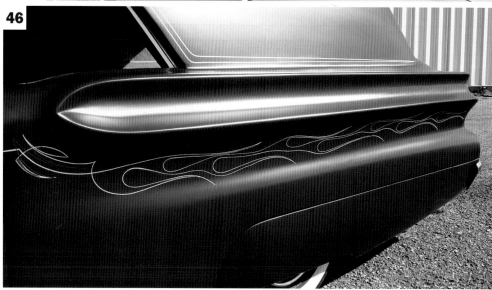

42 Look again. What first appears to be a shrouded sidepipe is actually not. The holes reveal there is no pipe behind the shroud. Instead, the false pipe starts near the back of the shroud.

43 "Smooth" was the key word on this custom 1941 Ford, originally built by Barris Brothers back in the late 1940s. The fenders were brought back, fadeaway fashion, and everything is either molded, smoothed, or rounded.

44 Dustin Cooper's 1955 DeSoto hardtop has long been a work in progress. The goal, the design, is to have a daily drivable, fully functional car that is also a custom. The top was chopped, and all working windows, including the rear quarter windows, were maintained.

45 The chop on this 1954 Mercury sedan included leaning the rear window forward, a smoothing and streamlining move. The new, smaller rear window was set in place with rubber gasket, making the car usable as the owner does more work.

46 No, Mercury didn't produce a sedan delivery in 1957. The company did make a cool two-door hardtop wagon, though. This one's been converted to the former. Along the way, it lost a lot of excess chrome trim. Part of the smoothing process on this car was to flush fit the cruiser fender skirts, which is a really nice touch.

47 The Matranga 1940 Mercury made this style of rear quarter windows popular. The curved front edge where the B-pillar used to be makes the car look like it's moving even when it is not. Most of these windows are fixed in place like this one. They can also be made to slide in via a channel.

48 After it was involved in an accident, this Chevy coupe was converted to the three-window *High School Confidential*-style by Dave Pareso at Back Street Kustoms in Colorado Springs. The original *HSC* movie cars were built at the Barris Brothers shop in Lynwood, California.

49 Nothing says style and craftsmanship better than a perfectly blended yet removable hardtop. Dick Bertolucci and Harry Westergard both had a hand in this one. Notice how uniform the minimal gap is between the body and the top. That is some beautiful work.

50 Built in the early 1960s, this 1958 Ford follows that style very well. It has a metalflake paint job and custom boat-style seats with a bar between. Dual sidepipes, spotlights, and enhanced fins all fit the bill.

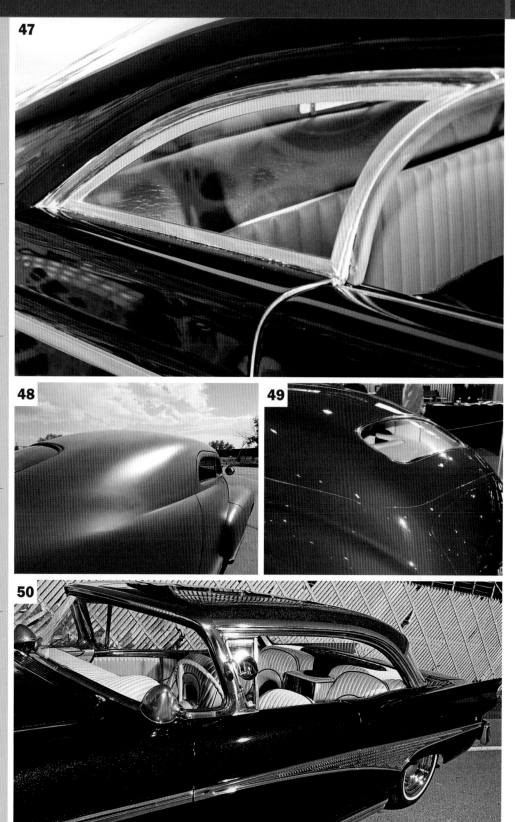

51

51 Barris' *Aztec* uses scoops and sections of perforated metal in its somewhat garish and flamboyant style. There's also lots of chrome. This is one of Barris' Hollywood-style cars; a bit over the top for the average guys but popular on the indoor show circuit.

52 Sometimes a car owner or builder will use features of a car to showcase his or her business. That's the case with Ms. Metal's 1953 Chevy and its spider web "fender skirts." She makes such accessories as shift knobs, car-related jewelry, and spider web headlight covers.

53 The triple shorty sidepipes on the *Kopper Kart* clone are duplicates of the original truck's pipes. They stylishly fill the place where small steps for the Stepside bed once stood.

54 There's a fine line between lowriders and customs. This 1961 Cadillac straddles the line. It's mostly shaved and lowered. It sports Bellflower exhaust tips, wire wheels, custom paint on the roof, and hydraulic or Air Ride suspension.

52

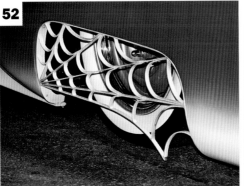

53

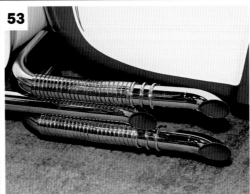

54

55 The builder of this 1949 Ford created his style with the coved, sculpted wheelwell arches flowing into the fenders. They break up an otherwise slab-sided body surface.

56 The stainless-steel or chrome strips on the roof of a 1957 or 1958 Buick Caballero station wagon could be adapted to other similar station wagons, resulting in a custom look using factory parts. There are actually still cars with these parts intact in old junkyards.

57 A popular 1950s style, but not seen much since, was this application of running the chrome exhaust pipes out from under the car at the back of the rocker panel and then up over the fender skirts and out the back.

Chapter 7
Chassis & Drivetrains

When building a custom car, keep the overall theme of the car in mind. A custom is a smooth, sleek, classy ride. A smooth-running engine and comfortable ride are parts of that overall package. You'll never regret a decision that leads to reliable and pleasant drivability.

In the early 1950s, Cadillac and Oldsmobile overhead valve V-8s were a popular swap. By the mid-1950s, Studebaker, Packard, Ford, Lincoln, Mercury, Pontiac, and Buick also had OHV V-8s, so those are engines to be considered. For a period nostalgic feel and look, early inline six-cylinder engines are good too.

As in most types of modified cars these days, the small-block Chevy engine is king. It's the most plentiful engine available since it's been in production in America's favorite car brand for well over 50 years. But there are several other viable alternatives too.

Regarding transmissions, either automatic or manual transmissions can be utilized. Vintage transmissions can be rebuilt with new parts. Additionally, a few companies like Bendtsen's Transmissions of Ham Lake, Minnesota, make adapter kits to put a modern Chevy manual or automatic overdrive behind most vintage engines.

Customs should sit low for best effect. Air-assisted suspension offers the choice of sitting low and cool when parked and then quickly raising the car up to a more reasonable ride height when driving. Shortened coil springs and lowered leaf springs (by re-arching, getting new springs, or using lowering blocks) offer the lowered look, but in a one-height version. That route is less expensive than Air Ride, though. It's a good idea to rebuild the suspension with new bushings, tie-rod ends, etc. in either case.

1 through 3 The Air Ride Technologies air bag system on the author's 1961 Pontiac allows different, infinite heights. It is also programmable to allow three different preset "automatic" heights instantly reachable by pushing one button. The lowest stance shown is with the air bags completely deflated. This would be the stationary car show stance but not suitable for driving. The second photo shows the most often used driving and cruising height, lower than stock but still manageable for most business driveways and most road conditions. The third photo shows the car raised substantially, as would be useful for clearing a steep driveway, loading onto a trailer, etc.

4 Raising and lowering a car via air bags changes the front end geometry, as shown on this 1941 Lincoln dropped to its lowered position. It's important to have the front end aligned with the car sitting at the normal driving height so as to not cause undue wear on suspension components and tires. Fronts can also be lowered by use of shortened or cut springs, or dropped spindles.

5 This is a typical custom's tail dragger stance with the front end a little higher than the back. Customs look strange with the rear higher. Several methods can be used to reach the desired height. Rear leaf springs can have lowering blocks installed, in effect raising the axle further above the springs. For coil spring suspensions in the rear, shorter coils can be used or coils can be cut. Do not heat and bend the spring; it takes the temper out of it.

6 Wheels and tires are an important part of the look of a custom. John D'Agostino gets his smooth chrome reverse wheels and Shannon cones like these on his *Golden Star* 1957 Olds from Pete Paulsen in California. They add a clean, uncluttered, and classy look. The wide whitewall tires are from Coker Tire Company in Chattanooga, Tennessee.

7

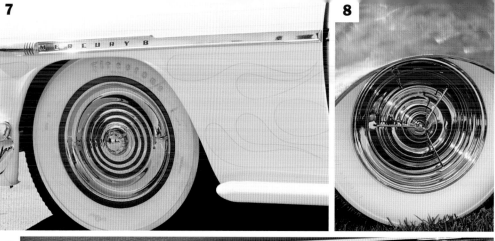

8

9

10

11

12

7 Coker Tire reproduces tires like the Firestone Deluxe Champions on Geno DiPol's Mercury from the original molds. The company also has U.S. Royal, B. F. Goodrich, and other brands, as well as its own. The wheel covers on this car are 1956 Oldsmobile covers, rechromed and painted with red rings to match the wheels.

8 Another variation on the smooth chrome wheels, these have a center cap to which a long, thin three-bar spinner has been added. The smooth chrome wheels are very versatile, changing appearance drastically with the different center caps.

9 Kirk Jones' 1960 Ford Starliner wears chrome wheels, too, but with the center section painted to match the car and with chrome spiders covering the center hub and lug nuts. The chrome spiders were a popular early 1960s accessory, now being reproduced in Ford, Chrysler, and GM bolt circle sizes.

10 Brian Everett went the naked route on his chrome wheels. Rather than spiders or caps, he used a chrome center grease cap and chrome lug nuts; a very traditional approach.

11 Mag wheels like these Radir Wheels' replicas of Mickey Thompson's old Rader Wheels are really better suited to hot rods and muscle cars than customs. They're too sporty or racy rather than classy, the look most people are going after with a custom.

12 It's only natural that Cadillac wheel covers are among the most desired for customs. Cadillac was the "standard of the world" when customs were in their heyday in the 1950s. Here are 1952 Caddy covers to which center bullets have been added.

13 Another very popular Cadillac wheel cover is the one from 1957. Because of their design featuring many ribs that strengthen the cover, as well as prevent dents, they seem to have survived in greater numbers and are relatively easy to find in good condition.

14 and 15 Cadillac covers from 1947 to 1952, commonly known as sombrero covers because of their shape, are among the most sought after, probably because they were used by early important customizing pioneers like Sam Barris. Understandably, a lot of them were dented, but they can be repaired. It's no wonder they are so popular, though, as they really dress up an early car.

16 These wheel covers appear to be 1953 to 1955 Oldsmobile Fiesta covers with a Mercury head crest added to the center. Olds Fiesta covers are being reproduced, too, but the real ones like these are much more desirable.

17

18

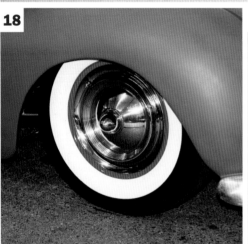

19

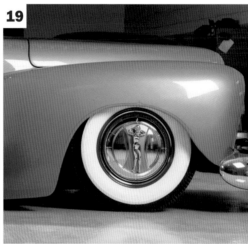

20

17 Wire wheels (real ones, not wheel covers) became popular in the early 1960s. Among those usually chosen for Ford products were ones from 1962 to 1964 Thunderbirds like these. A few good originals remain, but the wheels are also being reproduced.

18 We're not sure what the origin of these covers is, but they look great. The combination of a bullet center (seemingly added on), ribbed surfaces, and smooth ones really adds depth to the covers, but they are simple enough to not detract from the car.

19 "Naked lady" center bars were an accessory available in the 1950s from places such as J. C. Whitney and Warshawsky's. They are currently being reproduced, and a set showed up on "Voodoo" Larry Grobe's *Voodoo Idol* Ford coupe. Larry has attached them through the wheel covers to the hub so that they do not spin when the wheels turn.

20 Single bar flipper wheel covers were popular in the late 1940s and early 1950s, especially on customs from that era. These covers are on a 1939 Ford convertible owned by actor John Spencer and built by Dave Kinnaman of Kinnaman's Kustom Kars near Alexandria, Indiana.

21 As it is with hot rods, the venerable and sturdy small-block Chevy engine is the most often used one in custom cars today. They are plentiful, reliable, powerful, and easy to get parts for. Geno DiPol's 1949 Mercury, *Dixie Deluxe*, has one that's been hot rodded a little bit and also has ribbed Corvette valve covers and chrome "ram's horn" exhaust manifolds (both from Speedway Motors).

22 Pretty, huh? It's hard to beat multiple carburetion for a great look under the hood, though it would probably deliver about four times the needed fuel! Customs are usually meant more for show than go, so many times guys who run multiple carbs will not hook all of them up. It prevents drivability headaches.

23 This Ford flathead with three carbs is dressed up with lots of matching ribbed aluminum speed equipment and accessories, including Offenhauser heads. It also has a Vertex magneto.

24 Lynn Draper's 1961 Chevy Impala is running a Chevy 348 engine, recognizable by the dual hump cutouts in the heads and valve covers. He also has a 1950s Oldsmobile air cleaner. Cadillac made a similar one that was larger.

25

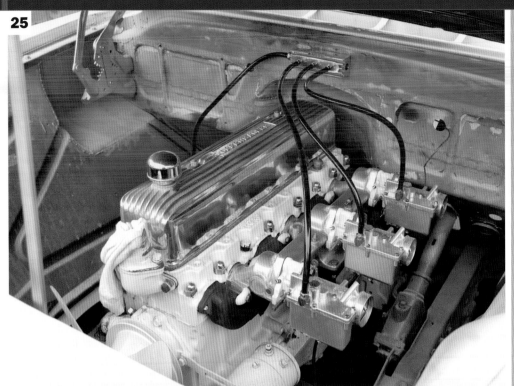

25 Chevy and GMC six-cylinder engines were mostly unchanged except for displacement for decades. They were available in sizes up to 302 cubic inches (GMC), so they can put out some decent power. Being inline sixes, they also have good torque. That's why they were used in trucks for so long. They are great for early Chevy customs.

26 The Chevy sixes are good looking engines, too—good enough to be run in a hot rod custom without a hood. They can be dressed up with chrome and with period speed equipment and are still stone reliable. Add a five-speed manual or four-speed automatic for economy.

26

27

27 Pontiacs deserve Pontiac power. The 1960 *Golden Indian*, owned by Lou Calasibetta, has the stock 389 engine with tri-power (three two-barrel carburetors). That's the standard Pontiac blue engine color for that era. Note how neat and clean the engine compartment is. It's not flashy, but if someone wants to see the mill, it still looks nice.

28

28 Buick V-8 engines like this "Nailhead" are also good upgrade engines for customs of lower market stature (Fords, Plymouths, and Chevys, for instance). The engine puts out great torque and places like Egge Machine have all the parts needed to rebuild one.

29 Though most custom cars are shown with the hoods closed so as to not break up the lines of the car, a little under-hood dress-up cannot hurt. This Offenhauser valve cover on a six-cylinder Chevy has been painted to match the purple metalflake roof on the car (see chapter 10). The owner, a pinstriper herself, has added some of her craft to the firewall too.

30 Torque monster Cadillac engines are the ultimate powerplant upgrade to most customs. In the early days of customs, Cadillac was everyone's aspirational car brand, so adding components to one's "lesser car" was always the way to go. Some guys would be happy with just the air cleaner!

31 "Thunderbird" was a magic word for Ford guys back in the late 1950s. One of the reasons was the 312 Y-block V-8, like in this 1957 T-Bird. Even if the whole engine didn't go, the Thunderbird valve covers often wound up on lower displacement Y-blocks in custom Fords.

32 Yeah, it's got a Hemi. This is a 1957 DeSoto Hemi, but they were offered in various Chryslers, DeSotos, Imperials, and Dodges. They were as popular back then as they are now. There are still some around. Be prepared to pay handsomely for a good one or to spend a lot rebuilding a worn-out one.

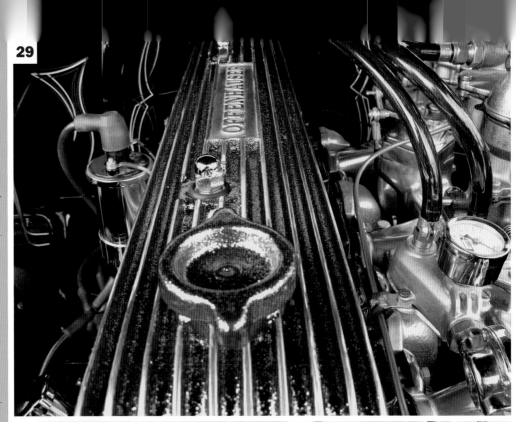

33

36

33 There are plenty of good Chrysler engines available besides Hemis, though, and they come in many different displacements. Like Chevy and Ford engines, they are available in junkyards, as well as from dealers in crate motors. There are dress-up and hop-up parts aplenty, too, like this dual four-barrel intake manifold.

34 The 352-cubic-inch FE series engine was standard on the 1958 Thunderbird and available on some other Fords. The well-known 390 and 406 engines were from the same family. It's a heavy engine but puts out good torque and can be made to run pretty strong. The famous Police Interceptor engines were FE series motors. Ask someone who tried to outrun one what they'll do!

35 The engine that made Oldsmobile famous, the Rocket V-8, was introduced in 1949 and became an instant hit. It was light, offered great power, and came out six years before Chevrolet and Pontiac OHV V-8s, four years before Ford's. It was the hot ticket. It still is for a cool nostalgic engine.

36 Here's a good look at a Chevy 409 (same block as a 348) going into Chris Pareso's 1940 Mercury custom, being built for her by her husband, Dave, at his Back Street Kustoms shop in Colorado Springs, Colorado. The 409 and 348 are good engines for heavy customs because they offer a good deal of torque.

37 Here's what most customs look like under the hood: pretty nondescript. Customs are made to look good, and the flow of the body lines dictates that the cars be displayed with the hood, trunk, and doors closed. As such, most guys spend their money on the outside and the interior rather than paying to dress up an underhood that few people will see.

38 Studebaker, one of the independent car manufacturers, had its own OHV V-8 engine in 1951, before everyone but Cadillac and Oldsmobile. Parts are still available for them, and they're good engines. This is the author's 1952 Commander custom project with its good running stock engine, which will remain the powerplant of choice for the finished car. It's backed by a three-speed manual transmission with overdrive.

39 Gene Winfield's *Maybelline* 1961 Cadillac is powered by a late-model, fuel-injected, dual-overhead cam Cadillac Northstar V-8. Notice how low it sits in the car, making it a good but complicated engine for cars with low hood heights or ones that have been sectioned.

40 and 41 Here are a few ways to dress things up under the hood if you are so inclined. Chrome is always a good choice, and it is easy to clean too. Pinstriping and a few graphic items like a flying eyeball also work. The underhood area of Geno DiPol's Mercury features striping and art by Junior Huff. Bo Huff added the flamed cutout cover to cover the hole around the steering column and where the shift lever rod used to come through the firewall.

Chapter 8
Front Ends

To be attractive to most custom car aficionados, the car needs to look right from every angle. This is nowhere more important than on the front end. That's not just looking straight on from the front either. It needs to look good from every angle, whether the viewer is looking from 20 degrees to the side, stooping down at eye level, or standing up.

We mentioned in chapter 6 the importance of style and flow. Well, the flow starts at the front. When you view a car, it's almost always from the front first, whether seeing a car coming toward you on the street or at a show or parked in a lot. Watch at a car show as people come up to a car for the first time. Even if they approach from the rear, they'll walk to the front and check it out. Then if the car interests them, they'll walk and view down the sides and then at the rear. The whole picture in our minds starts with the front end.

That's why the front end appearance is so important. It's like the face on a human being. It tells the car's personality. To borrow from an old adage, when building a custom car, put your car's best face forward.

1 John Spencer's 1939 Ford custom has a tastefully done Packard grille, Frenched headlights, and no front bumper. The car was built by Dave Kinnaman in Alexandria, Indiana, and Gary Minor in California added the Packard grille.

2 Dave Pareso's Studebaker truck has a grille filled with hood spears from a 1957 Chevy . . . 24 of them. They sit in a custom, molded grille shell. The hood corners have been rounded. The headlights are from a 1962 Chrysler.

3 The Oz Customs–built *Golden Star* 1957 Oldsmobile owned by John D'Agostino has a lot more work done than is first apparent. In addition to the 1958 Buick grille set inside the stock Olds bumper, the front fenders have been extended and peaked. Headlight rims were peaked to match. This is a great example of how the front end sets the tone for the rest of the car (see the entire car in the Introduction).

4 *El Matador*, the 1940 Ford built by Bill Cushenbery and restored by Murphy & the Striper, has a perforated mesh grille punctuated with lengths of stainless-steel, teardrop-shaped tubes. The canted Lucas-style headlights are also set in a similar mesh. The front end is all molded and protected by chrome nerf bars.

5 Utah customizer Bo Huff is building this long-term project 1951 Mercury in his spare time between customer jobs. It has a totally custom front end treatment using upside-down 1962 Chrysler canted headlights, a custom-formed grille opening with single bar grille, and a molded bumper with bullets.

6

7

8

9

10

6 and 7 An example of upgrading in building a custom is Bill Hines' *Buddha Buggy* 1959 Chevy, which utilizes the grille, headlights, and bumper sections from a 1959 Chrysler Imperial. Hines also filled the fender/hood leading edge scoops and grilles, but he added dished scoops to the tops of the fenders, and also put scoops outside the outboard headlights.

8 This early 1950s Chevy is getting the full custom treatment. Individual staggered headlights, a custom grille shell with 1960 Cadillac grille, flared and molded fender lips, rounded hood corners, and Buick portholes in the hood are visible here.

9 Gordy Brown's salmon-colored 1954 Ford Victoria Skyliner (glass top) is a study in craftsmanship and smoothness. The custom one-piece bar grille looks like a natural. The car is nosed, hood corners are rounded, and headlights are molded in.

10 It's easy to see why 1955 Pontiac grilles are so popular with customizers of 1950s cars. This 1954 Mercury combines the Pontiac grille with a rolled pan and a shaved and peaked hood.

11 Simpler is usually better on a custom. Removal of the twin grille bullets on this 1951 Ford really cleaned up the front end. By itself, the stock wide grille bar is much smoother and less cluttered.

12 Every once in awhile, one of the factory designers got it right, leaving little or no room for improvement. The 1962 Pontiac Grand Prix is an example of such near perfection. The whole car was nearly a custom as it came from the factory.

13 Barris' *Blue Danube* Buick (this is Jack Walker's clone) used a pair of Cadillac bumper ends on either end of a bar grille, which is housed in a molded opening. A peaked rolled pan, rounded hood corners, and hooded headlights also are a part of this front end.

14 There is no cleaner designed grille than the one from a 1960 Mercury. It has been used on hundreds of customs. This is famed builder Bill Hines' 1959 El Camino. Following the smoothed theme of the grille, he also filled the "eyebrows" above the grille and rounded the hood corners— classically tasteful.

15 Here's John D'Agostino's 1961 Oldsmobile with a 1960 Mercury grille. The Merc grille looked like a custom grille as it came from the factory, so it really works well in late 1950s to early 1960s cars. Another plus is that a lot of people don't recognize what it's from because 1960 Mercs are not very plentiful.

16 This is another variation on the same grille in the same model of car. This is Richard Zocchi's 1961 Oldsmobile, but rather than the Mercury headlights, he used 1960 Buick headlight housings. The result is a completely different look.

17 This is another John D'Agostino 1961 Oldsmobile treatment, this one a Starfire convertible built by Bill Hines and Oz Welch. Hines used one of his favorite grilles, that of a 1959 Chrysler Imperial, for a bold look.

18 One of the more popular mid-1950s grilles to use in customs is that of the 1955 DeSoto. This car is actually a 1955 Chrysler with the entire front clip of a 1955 Desoto utilized. If it's good enough for customs, it's good enough for (nearly) stock.

19 Speaking of 1955 DeSotos, Dustin Cooper from Avon, Indiana, kept the stock grille in his car but removed the front bumper guards, which also support the grille on the stock application. The result is completely different look. It makes people scratch their heads because they know it's familiar but different.

20 One of the few times when you might want to consider going backward in age regarding the grille for an early-style custom: The 1936 Cadillac grille works wonderfully on this 1940 Chevy, adding elegance and class. It's a great look. Cadillac and similar LaSalle grilles are somewhat plentiful and a good choice.

21 In the 1950s, Detroit's Alexander Brothers owned the franchise on tasteful customs cars. The *Golden Chariot* 1956 Chevrolet, owned and restored by Lou Calasibetta at Old Stillwater Garage in New Jersey, is a prime example. It has a full-width floating bar grille with simple round parking lights behind it.

22 The smoothest of the 1946 to 1948 Chevy front ends was the 1946 with its horizontal bar grille. The builder of this Chevy from that era has taken two 1946 grille housings and combined them into one clean oval with bars. He's also cleaned up the front with Frenched headlights and parking lights.

23 The center grille bar from 1953 Oldsmobiles makes its way into the cavities of many late 1940s to early 1950s customs. It's easy to see why when looking at this 1953 Olds. The owner has wisely kept the stock grille and has shaved most of the remaining trim. The headlights are Frenched.

24 One of the most famous faces in custom truckdom is that of the *Kopper Kart*, the Barris Kustoms shop truck. This is the clone, owned by Vic Collins and built at Mark Wojcik's Customs by Flash shop in New Jersey. The front end is a combination of a custom grille, rolled pans, mesh, and copper plating.

25

25 Gary Meyers' 1959 Chevy El Camino resides in Darryl Starbird's museum in Oklahoma. The El Camino has a pancaked hood, custom blade-style bar grille in a reformed opening, headlights behind flat plastic panels, and a rolled pan with custom bumperettes.

26 Richard Zocchi's 1939 Dodge coupe has been around for several years. Wearing canted headlights, a LaSalle grille, and scallops and striping by Art Himsl, it's one of the nicest early Mopar customs ever built.

27 Give up? It's the center part of a 1951 Packard grille, set in an early 1950s Chevy. The grille opening has been reshaped to follow the contours of the Packard grille. As natural as this one looks, it's a wonder more folks don't use Packard grilles. It's a great and different look.

28 The front end on Bill Cushenbery's *Limelighter* 1958 Chevy, owned by Bud Millard, is custom all the way. The headlights are tunneled into scalloped and extended fenders. The custom rolled pan and grille opening surround a perforated mesh grille with a single center bar. The whole front end is smoooooth!

26

27

28

29 The full custom bar grille on Mark Wojcik's 1961 Dodge is obvious, as is the Larry Watson–inspired panel paint job. Less obvious is the pancaked and rounded hood with louvers at the rear corners. Also check and consider that front bumper. It's stock to the Dodge, but it would look great on any number of other custom cars.

30 and 31 Perhaps one of the best stock designs to ever come out of Detroit, the 1960 Pontiac was really hard to improve upon. The Alexander Brothers did it better than anyone with their *Golden Indian*. The front end features a horizontal bar grille, and parking lights are in the ends of the lower bar. The sunken headlights are in perforated metal tunnels. The rolled pan tapers in from the sides.

32 This late 1940s Ford has a grille from a 1949 Dodge. The cars are similarly shaped in the front so it's a natural fit, giving a completely different custom look to the Ford. Peaked headlight bezels and fenders help the look too.

33 Darryl Starbird's iconic *Predicta*, based on a 1956 Ford Thunderbird, is all custom from one end to the other. The front end is no exception with its tube grille, dual headlights behind flat plastic, canted fender lines, and custom oval grille opening.

34

35

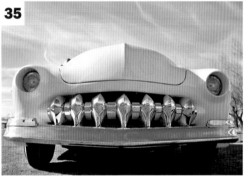

36

37

38

34 One wonders if there is a 1953 DeSoto anywhere that still has its grille teeth. Most seem to have been pilfered for custom 1949 to 1951 Mercurys. They fill the cavity nicely, and it's hard to beat their shiny and toothy chrome smile.

35 There are viable and very attractive alternatives to the DeSoto grille. Bo Huff used a 1951 Ford pickup grille with two extra teeth in Geno DiPol's 1949 Merc. Note how he molded the ends of the grille bar into the end of the cavity. Bumpers on this car are from a 1954 Pontiac with Deluxe guards on the ends.

36 Barris' 1955 Chevy-based *Aztec* uses every trick in the book. It has dual scooped headlights, hood scoops, a perforated mesh grille with a floating bar, a rolled lower pan with a 1957 DeSoto-style bumper—also filled with mesh and a bar—above it, molded scallops and peaks on the hood, and pinstripes. And chrome—lots of chrome.

37 & 38 This is another Richard Zocchi masterpiece: a 1964 Pontiac Grand Prix. The Grand Prix is an elegant design stock. Zocchi has extended the front fenders slightly past the bumper and put a split in the sides to house the Frenched stacked headlights. The grille is a custom closely stacked bar grille. Otherwise, the front end received a clearing of emblems, and that was about it.

39 Dan Keene's 1955 Dodge station wagon has a custom-molded grille shell and a split 1955 Chrysler grille bar. It's been nosed, and the two-tone paint follows the car's natural lines. The headlight rings are from a 1955 Oldsmobile and sit in front fenders extended 3¼ inches.

40 George Kilger's *Gator* 1951 Chevy is a genuine back-in-the-day custom. It sports a handmade front nerf bar/bumper, 1955 Chevy headlights (very popular in 1955 for customs), and a DeSoto grille in a reshaped and molded grille cavity. The hood is shaved, peaked, and the corners rounded.

41 Another Bo Huff Customs Mercury, this one has canted 1958 Lincoln headlights (wider chrome rims than Chryslers), 1955 Pontiac bumpers set into a molded gravel pan, and a 1957 Buick grille set into an oval cavity. The hood corners were rounded, and the angle on the front hood matches the angle of the headlights.

42 The 1959 Imperial grille set into the grille cavity of this 1958 Ford seems a natural transformation. The cavity has been molded, and the car has had all emblems shaved. Additionally, the stock Ford hood scoop has been removed.

39

40

41

42

43

43 This orange Mercury was built by Jason Graham in Portland, Tennessee. It features a 1949 Merc grille with a custom insert replacing the vertical center bar. That's housed in a molded cavity. A ribbed bumper in a molded pan, top and bottom, finishes off the front.

44 This 1957 Chevy has been changed quite a bit, although it retains the stock front bumper. The two hood missiles have been removed and the holes filled. The other hood trim is shaved too. The grille bar is from a 1953 Oldsmobile, and the trademark 1957 Chevy headlight rings have been replaced with a smooth, Frenched treatment.

45 The use of two 1955 Chrysler grille bars gives Dave Pareso's 1951 Mercury a different look, although the grille opening itself is near stock configuration. The headlights are from a 1953 Buick.

46 One has to be very careful when customizing a really classic production design like a 1953 Studebaker. Near perfect from the factory, they're easy to mess up. This one is nice with a molded grille shell and a simple single bar in each side. The lights are Frenched.

44

45

46

47 and 48 Corvette grilles from 1953 have long been popular swaps, especially into Chevys like the 1950 from Great Britain. The grille shell is the stock Chevy one, and parking light lenses are aftermarket clear versions of the 1959 Cadillac style.

49 What a difference a grille makes! Other than nosing (removal of chrome on the hood), the only change to the front of this 1952 Ford is the installation of a 1957 Buick grille in place of the stock one. It totally transformed the car.

50 Bill Hines has a knack for using forgotten production parts that completely change the look of the car on his customs. Here he's used what appears to be a Chrysler Imperial rear bumper on the front of his 1957 Lincoln. The headlights are stock and the hood corners have been reshaped. The grille is a custom bar grille by Hines.

51 The bumper on this Ford truck is a 1958 DeSoto grille bar. The headlights are the popular 1962 Chrysler canted lights but turned upside down. The grille is fine mesh to which dozens of chromed heavy-duty coat hooks or stylized door pulls have been bolted on from behind.

52 On the other hand, sometimes simple does the trick. This early 1950s Chevy has a plain oval grille opening with a single bar wearing bullets at each end. Some interest is added by molding a second ring around the grille opening. The headlights are Frenched and the hood has been shaved.

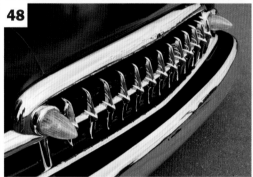

53

53 This 1950 Ford was sectioned, and so was its grille opening. A single floating horizontal bar fills it and looks just right. The hood was left stock height so it appears about the same height as the grille shell below it, making for a completely different look. The full sun visor adds a sinister touch.

54 Sometimes too much is just enough. The owner of this 1959 Cadillac added extra bars and bullets in what seems to be an attempt to make the car look as flashy and "in your face" as possible. Note even the flames going upward and diagonally rather than the usual front-to-back direction.

55 The front end on John Cooper's *El Tiki* show rod has a custom grille shell housing a mesh grille filled with the 1950s standard: chrome drawer pulls. Headlight housings are the front few inches of 1960 Buick front fenders. The car was originally built by Tom Culbertson of Indianapolis.

56 "Voodoo" Larry Grobe built his *Voodoo Idol* 1946 Ford as a tribute to Gene Winfield. The grille is from a 1947 Studebaker—who else would have thought of that? The front bumper overrider is from a 1954 Kaiser. The hood was custom made from scratch. The front bumper is from a 1949 Cadillac.

57 No, it's not an alien, but this Japanese Dodge Dart has a little of the look, helped immensely by the green teardrop-shaped headlight covers. A couple hundred small chrome bullets adorn the mesh grille.

58 The center section of the grille on this 1941 Ford has been filled in, leaving only the smaller two outside sections. The trim has been shaved, and the front bumper removed, leaving a smooth, rolled pan instead. If you cover a part of a grille, be sure the car's cooling system can handle the decreased airflow.

59 Believe it or not, this is a rare 1957 Mercury station wagon. The builder took a reverse route on the car, seemingly making it *less* distinctive. He removed the front part of the sheet metal and put a flat bar grille and 1957 Chevy front fender ends on it. The front bumper is from a 1959 Plymouth.

60 California builder Brad Masterson has this 1951 Chevy as his daily driver, and he's continually updating it. He's added a 1954 Pontiac center section to the grille and blended it neatly into the Chevy grille housing.

61 Here's a 1961 Cadillac with several subtle, inexpensive little touches to its front end. The grille is made up of hardware store chrome drawer handles with fender-top trim and spears across the front. The parking lights have chrome bullets added. The Caddy's fender trim remains, but the hood has been shaved.

Chapter 9
Rear Ends

Rear end treatments on custom cars are as important as any other factor. When you think about the impressions that a custom can leave on a viewer, especially as it drives by, the rear end leaves the last impression. As a bystander watches a low and cool custom drive by, he'll notice the front first, turn and watch as the car goes past, and then see the rear end last.

As mentioned in chapter 6, the car's overall appearance flows like a rocket or an airplane, the front beginning the impression that flows smoothly along the fuselage/body, and finishes with the rear. The rear end must look like it belongs with the rest of the car. All too often, car builders do not think their designs through, and the rear end seems to be almost tacked on as an afterthought. That's a shame because it can ruin an otherwise great car.

This chapter features some ideas based on what other guys have done with their cars, or as some thought, starters on what can be done with some excellent raw material. Learn to look at stock collector vehicles not only as a sum of their parts, the entire car, but also consider how their individual components, in this case rear end parts, could be adapted onto your next custom.

1 There's more work here on this 1953 Chevy than is first noticeable. The 1956 Packard taillights dominate the rear end but do not overlook the sunken and molded license plate, the molded-in gravel pan that extends over the Cadillac bumper, the exhaust through the bumper, and the flawless execution by Gary "Chopit" Fioto.

2 Another approach to the use of Packard taillights is shown here on Dustin Cooper's 1955 DeSoto. Instead of using the stock Packard chrome bezels, he Frenched the lenses into the extended fenders on the DeSoto and added a slight drooped peak at the top. It's a completely different look from Chopit's version in the gold 1953 Chevy.

3 *Limelighter*, the 1958 Chevy Impala built by Bill Cushenbery, has a radically but smoothly customized back end. The rear bumper has been replaced by a smooth, rolled pan, above which a ribbed horizontal section simulates a bumper. Between the two is a grille. The trademark Impala triple taillights give way to single, larger sunken round taillights, and the area below the trunk lid has been extended and fins flowed together.

4 The Alexander Brothers built the *Golden Indian* 1960 Pontiac when it was nearly new. They radically and tastefully restyled the rear, utilizing a large oval grille opening that they filled with a custom horizontal bar grille. They created semi-elliptical taillights with flat lenses decorated with dual white plastic bars. The A-Brothers were pioneers in the use of plastics in customs.

5 Darryl Starbird's bubbletop *Predicta* was based on a wrecked 1956 Ford Thunderbird. In the rear, it features large angled fins and is dominated by a deep, full-width oval cavity filled with a four-bar grille. It follows the similar theme of the front end, tying the whole car together cohesively.

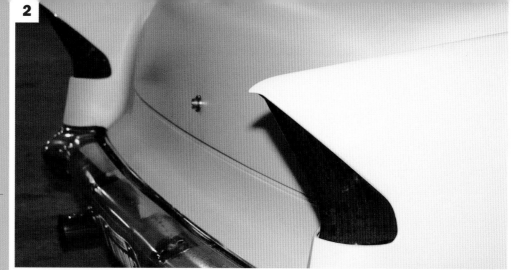

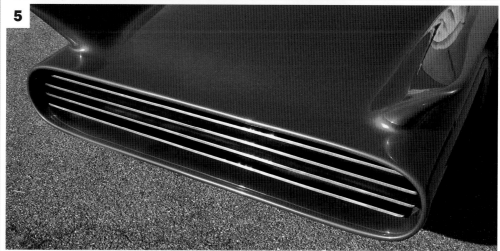

6 "Are they stock?" is the question most often asked about the 1961 Buick Invicta taillights Bo Huff and Rick Murray molded into the rear of the author's 1961 Pontiac. That's the mark of a successful custom application: It looks like it belongs. In reality, the Buick lights are about 50 percent wider than the stock Pontiac lights.

7 Dick "Peep" Jackson's 1957 Thunderbird, customized when new while he worked at the Barris Brothers shop, features custom taillight lenses, each made of two small lights and two bullets and mounted where the large round stock taillights were. The car also has plugs with Pontiac stars in the old bumper-end exhaust outlets. Bellflower exhausts run along the bottom of the rear quarter panels.

8 Chris Gomez's 1951 Kaiser is an unusual and worthy subject for a custom. Molded, sunken, and peaked Cadillac taillights; an Olds bumper; and a hand-formed continental tire bump in the trunk lid all add to its mystique. The car is one of the new crop of "unfinished" finished cars.

9 The rear end on this 1939 Ford custom, built by Dave Kinnaman, features molded-in custom taillights that create a very smooth flow on the fenders. The continental kit lays down and follows the lines of the trunk. The ribbed DeSoto bumpers are correct for a car styled in the 1950s motif.

10 Richard Zocchi's 1961 Oldsmobile has a top from a Ford Starliner and a Camaro back window. The rear panel has had the taillights taken out and is solid with a full-width chrome bar in it. Where are the taillights? They're in the clear ovals below the bumper. The bulbs are red.

11 *California Gold* is a 1951 Mercury built by Gene Winfield. The rear end treatment includes a 1955 Pontiac bumper overrider on the stock Mercury bumper. The rear fenders have been raised and extended, and each one features a pair of 1954 Packard taillights siamesed together to form a single lens.

12 General Motors built several Cadillac *Le Mans* dream cars for the GM Motorama in the early 1950s. This reworked one belongs to GM now and features flat fins reworked from original 1950s Cadillac-style ones. The taillights are similar to those on the 1960 Cadillac. A rolled pan with chrome ribs sits between Cadillac bumper ends with backup lights where the exhaust ports once were.

13 Another Alexander Brothers' creation is the *Golden Chariot* 1956 Chevrolet hardtop. Like the 1960 Pontiac, it belongs to Lou Calasibetta, who restored both cars in his Stillwater, New Jersey, shop, Old Stillwater Garage. The license plate is sunken into the deck lid. The rear quarter panels have been reworked and are angled and concaved on the end, holding custom flat taillights with plastic ribs.

14 Mostly stock on the rear end, this 1960 Ford Starliner has some touches of the A-Brothers' *Adonis*, including plastic ribbed taillights. The 1960 Ford rear end is a good example of a car whose components—flat horizontal fins, taillights, bumper—could be used on other cars. How about using the bumper and mounting the taillights upside down in it?

15 Though 1959 Chevys seem to be popular with customizers, 1960 versions like this one have similar lines and, at least in the rear, lend themselves more readily to customization. Several different taillights will fit in the concave section above the bumper. This car has a set of 1959 Pontiac Bonneville taillights, a perfect application.

16 Smooth and simple is often best. Take the taillights on this 1952 Buick. In their stock form, the lenses shown here reside in big and thick chrome housings that look tacked onto the ends of the fenders. Use the same lenses in custom housings Frenched into the fenders and it's a complete custom treatment.

17 Gary Brown, of Brown's Metal Mods in Indianapolis, built this Studebaker, and though it's not really a custom, the treatment on the bumper will work great for a custom. Brown narrowed the bumper ever so slightly and pulled it closer to the body, molding the whole thing in tight. It really cleaned up the back end, and the process would work on lots of different applications.

18 We give up on figuring out what these lights are from, but they look great on this early 1950s Chevy. Here's a perfect example of how transferring obscure parts to a different vehicle can result in a great custom treatment, and lots of observers won't know where they came from.

19 Here's another Gary Brown project, a 1951 Chevy Fleetline fastback. Notice how he has tapered the back into a boattail shape, a great idea that separates this car from all of the other 1949 to 1952 Fleetlines. The taillights are custom-formed red lenses in stylized fender cutouts.

20

20 Gary "Chopit" Fioto's 1949–1950 Mercury project features a narrowed mid-1950s Cadillac front bumper on the back of the Mercury. The gravel pan is extended out over the bumper, molding it in. Same with the extended lower rear quarter panels. The Dagmar bullets look wild on the back.

21

22

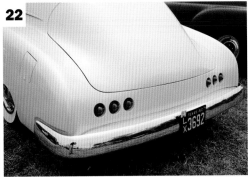

21 Some guys prefer suede and graffiti to shiny paint and chrome. The owner of this 1954 Chevy has allowed friends and car show acquaintances to autograph his trunk lid around the cool intricate pinstriped design in the middle. The taillights are Lee bubble-style lenses in painted stock housings.

22 This Chevy Fleetline has been shaved, and the stock taillight openings have been filled in. In the panel below the trunk lid, the builder has Frenched in three round bullet-shaped lights per side. It's a simple concept that works extremely well and still gives plenty of safe light.

23

23 Here's the right way to incorporate a continental kit onto a custom. Everything is smooth and molded in. The extended fenders are properly proportioned, and their curved extension follows the original fenders' downward slope. The gravel pan between the fenders and the bumper is also molded in. It looks like it belongs. Nothing looks tacked on.

24 The long, low 1954 Kaiser rear bumper overrider is a popular item with customizers and rightly so. It's very stylish with its length and the bullets at the end with concave centers. Its line makes the car look even wider, which is what we're after on a custom.

25 Who would have thought to use a 1958 Studebaker sedan rear bumper on a 1953 Chevy? Brian Zelenka of Chicago did. In true custom fashion, he extended the gravel pan to meet it and molded it in. The taillights might be a mystery to most folks too. They are from a 1955 DeSoto.

26 Taillights from a 1955 Lincoln look natural on this custom 1954 Mercury. The continental kit on this one rotates down electrically along with the center section of the rear bumper to allow access to the trunk.

27 Utah customizer Bo Huff is building a radical 1951 Mercury custom. The rear fenders utilize fenders from two 1951 Mercurys, and the severely chopped top flows into the inner pair of fenders. The rear bumper is made up of parts from four bumpers.

28 Oz Welch at Oz's Customs built this 1940 Mercury for Brian Everett. The rear features two large bullets and a handmade nerf bar/bumper setup. The taillights are twin round chrome motorcycle-style pieces mounted low on the nerf bar.

29 Mark Moriarity owns and restored this early 1955 Chevy custom. The rear end features 1955 Pontiac bumpers molded into the rear pan. The license plate has been sunken and is molded and scooped. The rear fender tops are capped, and the custom taillights are Frenched.

30 Chuck Fisher built Jerry Johnson this 1949 Ford business coupe. The list of modifications is a mile long and includes the scalloped rear fenderwells. The rear end of the car is dominated by taillights that are a combination of 1957 Plymouth lenses and 1962 Chevy round lights. The rolled rear pan has a bumper bar with backup lights set in the ends.

31 Amy Clark, a.k.a. Ms. Metal, owns and built this 1953 Chevy coupe. The extended rear fenders were finned, and then custom taillight housings were created. Into that went aftermarket 1959 Cadillac taillights, two on each side.

32 This one-off custom used many Kaiser parts but was actually built on a 1939 Dodge chassis in the 1950s. From this view are visible the LaSalle tire cover and DeSoto taillight lenses in Dodge trim. It was recently restored and was photographed at the Detroit Autorama.

33 This fastback Oldsmobile, similar in style to the Chevrolet Fleetlines, sports stock rear fender-top trim that stops at the newly Frenched and sunken round taillight tunnels, which house 1959 Cadillac lights. The rear deck has been shaved and the license plate sunken. Subtle metallic lavender paint is accented with purple pinstripes.

34 Packard taillights in extended fenders sit above a 1955 DeSoto rear bumper on Jake and Tammy Moomey's *So Low* 1954 Chevy. An uncommon modification is the deck lid, which has been sectioned 1.5 inches to take out some of its squareness.

35 Yenry Herrera went the Packard taillight route one better on his 1950 Chevy Fleetline, and it's a look that has custom guys smiling all over the West Coast. Yenry and Body Shop F-1 extended the rear quarter panels and turned the 1957 Packard taillights upside down and set them at an angle. It was a brilliant move.

36 This is Jack Walker's clone of Lyle Lake's 1952 Barris custom 1952 Buick. The rear bumper is from a 1953 Oldsmobile, and the exhaust flows through it. The Frenched taillight lenses are made up of two 1954 Mercury lenses each.

37 Rather than swap for taillights from a different car, the builder of this 1949 or 1950 Mercury molded his in. He added a raised, scalloped ring around the outside and accented it with pinstriping.

38 The world famous Hirohata Mercury was built for Bob Hirohata by the Barris Brothers shop in the 1950s. Its rear end is highlighted by 1952 Lincoln taillights set in the ends of the rear quarters, fully exposed as on the Lincoln rather than hooded as on many customs.

39 As though the purple metalflake paint didn't garner enough attention, this 1958 Ford also has extended and pointed tailfins and eight 1959 Cadillac taillights. The big chrome bumper is stock.

40 "Boston Bill" Dillman's 1959 Chevy El Camino has flat plastic taillight lenses replacing the stock ones. The tailgate has been molded shut, allowing the use of one-piece lenses rather than the split ones normally used on El Caminos and station wagons.

41 The Plymouth convertible is an early 1949 (same as a 1948). It features the highly desirable ribbed bumpers that came on the all-new 1949 Plymouth Second Series cars. This car also has a Carson top, Studebaker taillights turned 90 degrees and Frenched, and a sunken license plate under a scoop running up the trunk lid.

42 Bill Hines' 1949 Ford coupe known as *The Bat* has exaggerated fins, a Hines trademark, and round taillights set into their bases. The rear wheelwells are radiused, and there's a Kaiser overrider on the unidentified rear bumper.

43

44

45

43 *Lil' Bat* is Hines' 1980 Buick Riviera. It, too, has fins, as well as a split bumper and custom taillight housings. Set in the housings are Mercury Comet taillights.

44 The key to this 1940 Mercury convertible sedan (four-door convertible) is the craftsmanship. Originally built by Dick Bertolucci and Harry Westergard, it flows so perfectly. Note how the removable top fits with the rest of the body, even on the compound-curved rear quarters. Stock taillights are molded to the fenders, which are molded to the body.

45 Pickups can be very cool customs, and the same tricks work on them as on cars. This one has an oval rear cavity with two chrome bumper bars per side. The tailgate is molded closed, and a pair of custom taillights is Frenched into the top of the extended fender/ bed area.

46 The rear of "Voodoo" Larry Grobe's 1946 Ford coupe is impressive. A bumper from a 1949 Cadillac was molded in and wears a Kaiser overrider. Modified taillights are from a 1949 Plymouth. The rear quarters were extended, and a molded gravel pan was added between.

47 All the chrome trim was shaved from this 1960 Chevy. The trunk lid was extended out to the edges of the fins and down to the taillight panel, which is Frenched. Eight round taillights reside behind a full-width flat red plastic lens.

48 The rear quarters on this 1951 Mercury were extended and raised into fins. Residing in the fins are late-model Cadillac vertical blade-shaped taillights. The bumper was contoured to fit the extended quarters and notched for the taillights. Also note that the bumper overrider was molded into the bumper before it was chromed, making for a smooth one-piece assembly.

49

49 Cadillacs make great long and low customs, as evidenced by this 1951 model that has been made into a three-window coupe, exaggerating the long trunk area. The builder was taking smooth to the limits, though, by sealing off and molding in the trunk lid. Though it looks good, it will prove to be impractical because the only access to that extended trunk compartment is through the interior.

50

50 General Motors coupes from the 1940s make excellent tail-dragger-style customs in the Westergard vein. As seen on this 1940 Chevy, one reason is their rear shapes, which can flow smoothly from the chopped and smoothed top into the deck lid and along the fenders. Smooth is the key, as evidenced by the molded fenders, fender skirts, and gravel pan.

51

51 Gary Meyer's 1959 Chevy El Camino is wild. The tailgate is welded shut, and the tonneau cover is molded solid too. Though they retain a cat's-eye shape, the taillight housings are completely different from stock, holding flat plastic lenses covered with custom grillework. A two-piece thin blade bumper rides above a rolled pan. Exhaust runs through the pan.

52 This is the iconic *Rod & Custom Dream Truck*, which was a continuing project truck in the 1950s. It was customized over a couple years at various shops throughout the country. From the rear, note the canted fins, rolled pan, and molded rectangular rear grille/taillight section. The rear end was fairly radical for the time, but it shows that radical can still be tasteful.

53 This photo shows what kind of stock components are out there that can look great either on the as-designed application or with a little imagination on another completely different car. These are the stock taillights from a 1955 Chrysler, one of the many components from Chrysler Corporation's styling heyday of the 1950s. They look good here on a Chrysler with the trunk lid shaved and pinstriped, but they would fit many other cars with some work.

54 To the rear of Geno DiPol's (publisher of *Ol' Skool Rodz* and *Car Kulture DeLuxe*) 1949 Mercury, builder Bo Huff added a 1955 Pontiac bumper overrider and custom taillights set into Pontiac Deluxe bumper wings. This allowed the smoothing of the rear fenders. The result is very striking yet simple.

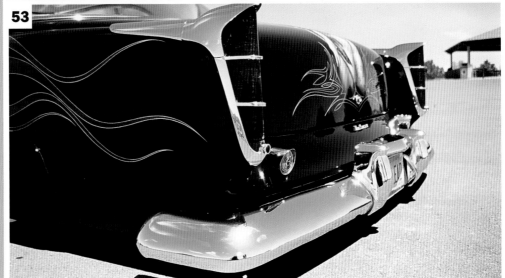

55 One modification often leads to another. When the builder of this Shoebox Ford added the extended grille housing to the rear of his car, he also had to section the deck lid to allow room for it. Frenched taillights are capped by peaked fender extensions. Original taillight flares on the sides of the rear quarters were left in place but rounded off and blended in.

56 Even usable trucks can be stylish. The owner of this mid-1950s Studebaker pickup has added some touches that do not detract from the utility of the truck at all. He has added a smooth outside skin to the bed and blended the fenders into it. Taillight housings were added to the ends of the bed rails and then extended straight down, adding some visual length to the bed. A car bumper finishes off the look.

57 Several custom legends had a hand in building this 1958 Chrysler, *Golden Sunrise.* Gene Winfield built the car, and it has been owned by Richard Zocchi and John D'Agostino. It was repainted by Art Himsl. The most recent owner added huge flamethrower cans to the rear, which do not fit the lines or personality of the otherwise classy car at all.

58 Taillights from a 1951 Dodge, which are a great simple design, were added to the rear fenders on this mostly hand-built custom coupe. The rear bumper is from a similar-era Chrysler product. Simple round backup lamps satisfy the law and fit well with this car's style, a simple one-off blending parts of numerous cars together well.

59 and 60 The rear end of Ron Gomez's 1941 Buick is a beautiful case study in smooth. The chrome trim, handles, and taillights have all been shaved. All components—gravel pan, fenders, rear deck body—have been flowed together tastefully. Custom-made taillights are housed in the rear bumper guards.

61 *Gator* is a 1951 Chevy coupe that appeared in *Hot Rod Magazine* in 1959. Its rear features completely reworked rear quarter areas, which have been lengthened and scalloped. In them are Frenched dual siamesed Packard taillight lenses. The quarters also have been scallop molded. The rear bumper was replaced with a rolled pan and a custom nerf bar–style bumper.

Chapter 10
Paint & Chrome

Beyond the actual design flow of a custom car, no other aspects define the car more succinctly than the chrome and the paint job. Sometimes it's a lack of paint and chrome. In any case, it's all about the appearance, the continuation, and final application of the car's style. Once all the bodywork and fabrication have been done and everything has been test-fitted, parts to be chromed are shipped off to the plating company, and the car heads for the paint booth. With all due respect to the tires, this is where the rubber *really* meets the road in a car build.

A few cautions about paint are in order. If you're not painting your car yourself, find the best painter you can afford. And that may not be the most expensive one. Ask around and find out about reputations. Ask friends or acquaintances how their paint jobs have held up over a few years. Body preparation for paint is even more important than the paint itself. Poor prep will begin to rear its ugly head fairly soon. It will show up as bubbles in the paint, cracks, or even chunks falling off. When that happens, the only way to fix it is to strip the car down to the bare metal and start over.

The same goes for chrome plating. Buy the best level of chrome you need, but don't overdo it. If your car is going for sweepstakes show wins, then show chrome is what you need. If your car is going to be driven quite a bit, you don't need that level. Again, ask around and look at other guys' chrome.

1 Try *not* to look at Richie Cordova's 1960 Cadillac Coupe de Ville. You can't do it. The lime green pearl paint and white scallops are perfect for the car. It has had just the right amount of chrome removed, and the right amount remains. This car was well painted and prepared and has stood up to thousands of miles of driving.

2 The flames on this 1954 Buick are just right. They are the right style for the rest of the car and they flow very nicely. Their layout actually visually lengthens the car, which has a squared-off shape.

3 Custom car legend Gene Winfield is also a painter in much demand. Car owners fly him cross country to paint their cars. This is his own *Maybelline* 1961 Cadillac, and it displays one of Gene's famous fadeaway paint jobs, his best known style. He's probably done hundreds over the years, and each one is a little bit different but still trademark Winfield.

4 This is one of Gene Winfield's well-known fadeaway paint jobs in progress on a 1949 Mercury four-door. It's being done at Winfield's shop in Mojave, California.

5 The Alexander Brothers were masters of color and chrome. The Detroit duo's 1956 Chevy, *Golden Chariot*, is a great example. The rich gold color relays elegance and class. They retained the right amount of chrome trim, modifying the stock side trim, and shaving the hood, rear deck, and doors.

6 Bo Huff describes the grille on Geno DiPol's 1949 Mercury as "like a DeSoto on steroids." Actually, it's a modified 1951 Ford pickup grille widened to fit the Mercury's grille cavity and with four teeth added to the original three from the truck. The teeth were chopped vertically, too, to fit the space. It adds a lot of chrome but doesn't overwhelm the 1953 Corvette ivory paint.

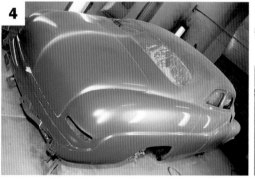

7

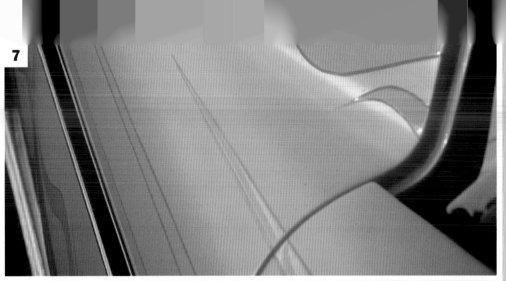

8

9

10

7 The paint on DiPol's Mercury is a combination of glossy and flattened 1953 Corvette ivory. The entire car was painted with the flattened version, and then Junior and Bo Huff laid out flames, which Bo painted with the glossy version. Junior outlined the flames with a gold pinstripe.

8 Yellow paint this bright might be too much for some folks, but it really works well on this 1951 Mercury from Indiana. It's contrasted with the commonly popular 1953 Buick side trim and white paint below. Note that almost all of the chrome on the car is down low, below the fenderline.

9 Cars from the 1950s were designed to be painted two-tone, so it carries over well in customs. Naomi Long's 1957 Plymouth, customized by Tom Culbertson, uses some stock trim and some adapted from other cars. The combo of gold metalflake and light charcoal works well.

10 To be such a bright color, this green Mercury by Oz Customs is really very tasteful. The thin metalflake scallops break up the expanse of green just right. Like most customs, this one's been nosed, decked, and shaved. The single bar grille and chrome bumper work to visually widen the car.

11 Another perfect Alexander Brothers execution is the *Golden Indian* 1960 Pontiac. The lime gold paint was a good choice, and the brothers retained some of the stock chrome/stainless trim. The inset side trim was actually done that way from the Pontiac factory, though current owner (and the car's restorer) Lou Calasibetta says people ask him if he Frenched it.

12 The 1951 Hirohata Mercury is probably the most famous custom Mercury of all time. Its two-tone green paint job has been copied on several cars besides Mercs. The car is so well done that it has been cloned, both in coupe and convertible forms.

13 Roger Odell's 1957 Cadillac Eldorado was painted by Larry Watson, one of the most famous and highly revered custom painters of all time. The car is two-tone rose and is accented by the chromed Eldorado-exclusive rear trim around the taillights and on the sides.

14 This is the car that made Larry Watson a household name among custom car fans all over the world: his 1958 Ford Thunderbird. Watson bought the car brand new and proceeded to shave the chrome and then custom-panel painted it. Here is where "customizing with paint" was invented.

15

16

17

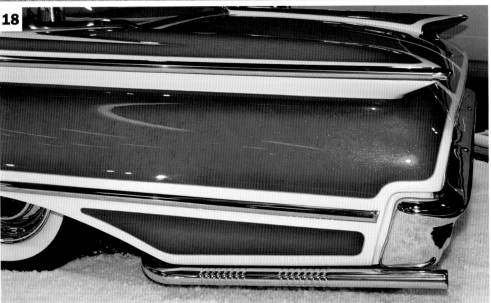

18

15 Another Larry Watson specialty was cobwebbing, which refers to evenly shooting thick paint in strings upon the car's panel. Not everyone can do it. Few can do it as well as Watson did. He painted this 1962 Thunderbird for his friend Gary Niemie.

16 One of Larry Watson's specialties is color. Here he's shown with a display he devised to show how paint reacts to light on curved surfaces. He built a display board and put lightbulbs in it, each painted in different shades of various candy and pearl colors. The result is more accurate than typical flat painted samples. That's why he's one of the best of all time.

17 Speaking of Watson, he didn't paint this 1961 Dodge. But Mark Wojcik of Customs by Flash in Howell, New Jersey, did, and he says that he was influenced by Larry's work. Mark retained the Dodge's front bumper but replaced the grille with a huge horizontal bar grille.

18 Kirk Jones' 1960 Ford Starliner has a fantastic combination of paint and chrome. The 1960s-style paint by Alex Gambino has a combination of metalflake, cobwebbing, scallops, and panels—all superbly executed. It's set off with most of the stock chrome, save the emblems, in place and rippled Bellflower tailpipes too.

19 Donnie Baird of Imperial Customs painted the body of his 1963 Oldsmobile Dynamic 88 a very subtle blend of lavender and lilac pearl with peak highlights of white pearl. Less subtle is the top, where he started with silver metalflake and then added a rose lace pattern in two shades of purple. On the C-pillars, he used the same colors and taped and sprayed a sunburst pattern emanating from the lower corners. Light charcoal borders the top.

20 The flamed purple metalflake top on Melissa Gee's 1949 Chevy Fleetline seems to flow over the car like its engulfing it from the top down. It's a striking concept. Note also that she has retained the polished beltline stainless trim, which balances with the chrome lakes pipes and bumpers on the lower part of the car.

21 Choice of color is especially important on a luxury car custom, such as a 1957 Cadillac Eldorado. Go too bright or garish and the tone of the whole luxury car custom is lost. This dark burgundy is just right, as are the wire wheels and the subtle top chop.

22 Taking a low-key approach to finishing a custom is also popular these days and usually reflects a low-buck custom with less attention to chrome plating, upholstery, and other luxuries. The primered 1955 Pontiac sedan shown here seems well done and has a clean engine bay and no hood. It's the anti-big buck version of customs.

23

23 Here's a suede (non-shiny) 1940 Chevy custom. With the suede cars, it's difficult to tell if the car is in transition and the owner is just enjoying it as he builds and saves more for the next finishing step, or if the car is in its finished version now. Either way, this is one cool custom.

24

24 Ron Gomez's suede 1941 Buick *is* finished. It features well-finished paint and very nice contrasting chrome. The 1941 Buick grille is a masterpiece and was a good choice to retain, as it fits the contours of the front better than a replacement could. The car was nosed and headlights Frenched, both serving to clean up the front end.

25

25 The author's 1961 Pontiac Ventura was built and painted by Bo Huff Customs in East Carbon, Utah. It features a lot of paint, as well as a lot of chrome work. The 1961 Pontiac was such a clean design as built that Bo decided to go mild with the body modifications and to mostly use chrome and paint to accent the car's lines and exemplary features.

26 The Pontiac's flared front bumper was retained but replated. The flames and scallops were laid out by Junior Huff, Bo's son (then 17). Both sides match, and he did it freehand. He also pinstriped around all the design, plus added a few pinstripe design touches in various places. Bo painted the car with lacquer, metalflake, candy, and ground glass. It sparkles in the sun.

27 Chrome may not "get you home," but it still looks good in the right places. The author's 1961 Pontiac got chrome added on the cowl vent and on the windshield inner trim. Also seen here are the chrome bullets put on in place of the wipers. They attach with a setscrew and are easily removed to refit the wipers.

28 Here's an unusual use of two-tone paint on a 1960 Pontiac: the colors split at the recessed chrome side trim. The builder has used the same silver and blue pallet to add stylized Indian heads on the side, as well as simple scallops. Barely noticeable are the light blue pinstriped flames in the silver above the color split.

29 A station wagon roof offers a big canvas for an artistic soul. On the roof of this Chrysler are a Maltese cross, flames, pinstriping, and lace-painted panels. The base car's body is beige, so the color is all on top.

30 Some guys prefer painted or powdercoated bumpers, grilles, and trim over chrome. It's not a universal trend, but it crops up once in awhile on cars like this 1953 Chevy. For traditional customs, chrome is still considered the preferred treatment by most custom fans and builders.

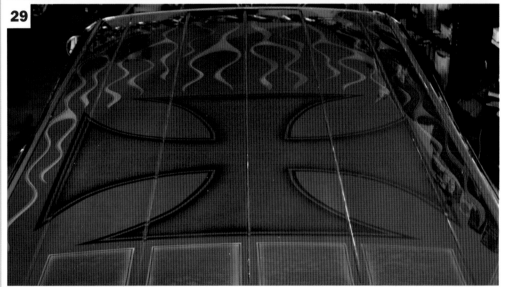

31 The word "subtle" has never been used to describe this Mercury. Photographed in Yokohama, Japan, at the Mooneyes rod and custom show, it definitely is covered in flames. On the lower section are parallel, diagonal airbrushed stripes. A paint job like this is a love-it-or-hate-it type of application.

32 Here is *Black Beauty*, Green Hornet's car created by Dean Jeffries for the *Green Hornet* TV series. "Black, black, and more black" was the theme of *Black Beauty*, which was better for Green Hornet and Kato to prowl around at night undetected, don't you know. This is really one car where the monochrome worked well. Credit Dean Jeffries for that.

33 This 1955 Plymouth has a simple looking but actually very complicated paint scheme. In the center are black-on-black, lace-painted panels. Around the outside of those are several sets of scallops, one outside the other, sprayed in a couple of different sheens or shades. Each successive scallop set is pinstripe outlined in gold.

34 Obviously Gene Winfield isn't the only master of fadeaway paint. The *Buddha Buggy* 1959 Chevy Impala was originally built by Bill Hines, and he restored it some 45 years or so later. It has a massive chrome 1959 Chrysler Imperial grille.

35 The *Car Craft Dream Rod* was originally built by Bill Cushenbery in the early 1960s. It is owned by Minnesotan Mark Moriarity, who recently restored it. The car features painted fogged highlights on body ridges, chrome sidepipes, a stripe on the side, and sparkling chrome wire wheels.

36 Brad Masterson of Masterson Kustoms of L.A. painted this 1951 Chevy sedan for fellow Beatnik Car Club member Jack Rudy. It's painted all one color: lime green metalflake. The fades and highlights were done with toner sprayed over the base metalflake. The side trim that resembles popular (and expensive) 1953 Buick trim was actually made by Brad from 1956 Chevy reproduction pieces.

37 Looks like paint, but it ain't! Avon, Indiana, customizer Dustin Cooper chopped the top on his 1955 DeSoto, and instead of repainting the top, he stripped off all the paint, polished the metal, and then sprayed it with clear to keep it from rusting. The same thing could be done in panels on a car's body, couldn't it?

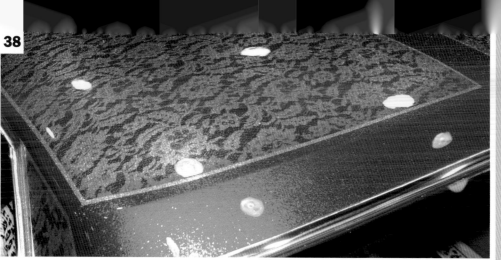

38 This one is Dustin Cooper's 1964 Cadillac Coupe de Ville. It has classic lace-painted roof panels over a silver metalflake roof. Though not shown here, the body of the car is plain white. Such a treatment as this one serves two purposes. It adds a custom touch to an otherwise mild car. It's also a fairly inexpensive way to add that touch, as the roof is small compared to the rest of the car, so it doesn't require much paint.

39 Though we're not condoning painting a car pink, pink pearl works pretty well on this 1954 Mercury. The car is built in a mid-1950s style, when such colors were inexplicably popular. Here it's highlighted with maroon scallops and small starbursts. Chrome rings around the Frenched headlights add a touch of shiny stuff.

40 If a little bit of metalflake is good . . . This Shoebox Ford is completely covered in the stuff. Note, too, that nearly all chrome is removed so it doesn't compete for the viewer's attention with the metalflake. Sidepipes and bumpers are down low, drawing the lowness even lower visually.

41 Here's an excellent example of "customizing with paint." The Oldsmobile is mostly stock, even retaining its stock grille and bumpers, but nosing and decking combined with a great panel paint job make the car seem more radically customized than it really is. This is a great application of paint.

42 This is actually a stick-on, but it's a fun way to add some variety to car without getting too seriously involved in paint. It's a great way to look cool driving down the highway with the driver's arm hanging out, even if it's raining!

43 Used in the right places, original chrome can be very effective. Geno DiPol's 1949 Mercury retains its side chrome (replated), and the recesses in the letters have been painted red to match the wheels, the rings in the 1956 Oldsmobile wheel covers, and the car's interior.

44 Gary "Chopit" Fioto is pretty adept at knowing how much chrome is just right and what color to put with it. The gold 1953 Chevy's grille opening was molded in and painted the body color, but the extra teeth added to the grille picked up the extra shine factor. Beltline trim remains, but the car was shaved, nosed, and decked.

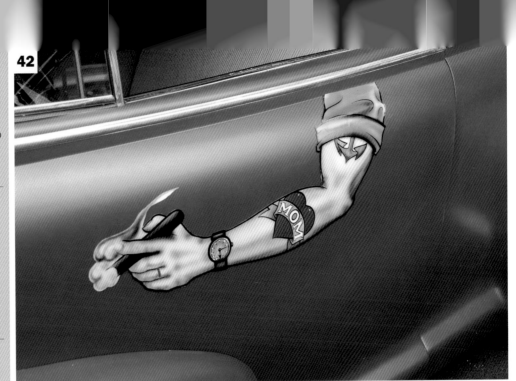

Chapter 11
Interiors

Creation of a great custom interior is an art. As sure as the craftsmen who sculpt the outside form of beautiful custom cars are artists, those who work in foam, leather, and vinyl are too. Though the interior is the last part of a custom build to actually happen, it should not be the last thing planned. The interior needs to follow the theme and style of the whole car. If it does not, the car will not be as attractive as it should have been. A mismatched interior will confuse the observer.

Since the owner spends much of his time inside the car, the interior should be attractive and comfortable. There's nothing

worse than taking a long drive in an uncomfortable seat. If you are building a new custom, get with your intended interior craftsman early so that you can plan your interior's features, budget for its cost, and get set into the interior shop's schedule.

As with all aspects of a custom build, check around and look at some interiors. Find out who did the ones you like. Interior craftsmen have certain styles, and most don't vary from their chosen style much, so pick someone whose style you like. You won't convert him to your style, and he'll do a better job on a style he's comfortable with.

1 The interior of Bill Cushenbery's *Limelighter* 1958 Chevy (owned by Bud Millard now) has a ton of great ideas. The radical twin pod "instrument panel" emanates from stalks off the steering column. There's a custom console with more gauges in a large pod. The steering wheel is from an Oldsmobile, about 1959 to 1960 vintage. Air conditioning vents are discreetly placed in the console too.

2 Technically this car is not a custom; it's a 1927 Essex hot rod built by Gary Brown at Brown's Metal Mods in Indianapolis. What's of interest to customizers is the instrument panel, the upper section of which is from a 1958 Edsel. Keep your eyes open, as there's a lot of this cool stuff on 1950s cars.

3 Individual rear bucket seats were very popular on 1950s and 1960s custom cars. This Canadian 1956 Chevy has followed the theme. A wide custom console separates the rear seats. The console mimics the contour of the outboard armrests. Contrasting colors make for a colorful interior.

4 Doug Corson of Classic & Street Rod Interiors in Grand Junction, Colorado, devised and built the interior for the author's 1961 Pontiac custom. The bucket seats and console are from a 1966 Pontiac Grand Prix. The rear seat is the stock one for this car. The black inserts have alternating pleats of two different grains of vinyl. Notice the inserts in the seats, console, and side panels?

5 and 6 The black inserts are removable and can be replaced with the white ones shown here, transforming the interior from black and white to all white. Obviously any other color could be used as well. Such an interior requires the upholsterer to make patterns for the various inserts and to be able to make two pieces alike repeatedly in order to pull off the ingenious design. The white inserts have pleats of alternating pearl- and matte-finished white vinyl.

7

8

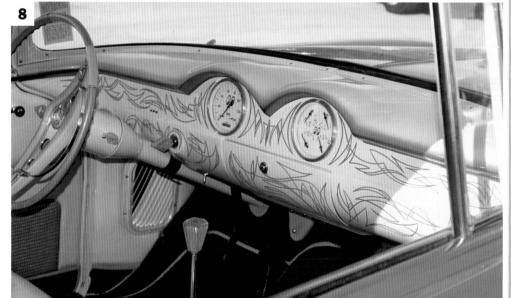

9

7 Chrysler products of the late 1950s to early 1960s had some of the most stylish interiors ever put in a car. They make great resources for adding cool touches to customs done in the styles of that era. This is a 1957 Imperial, and it's beautiful inside.

8 Here's a different spin on a 1956 Chevy interior, and it would work on lots of other cars too. The builder Jeff Myers took the two humped surfaces from each end of the top of the stock panel and moved them to the center. The glove box was already in the center, so it stayed there. Gauges were moved to the center also, and all the chrome trim was left off, replaced decoratively by pinstriping.

9 Here are the seats on the same 1956 Chevy, done up early 1960s-style by Fat Lucky's with white vinyl and blue piping to match the outside of the car. The pattern involves quite a bit of labor so is more expensive to make than a more straightforward design, but it really stands out.

10 Fat Lucky's Interiors in Austin, Texas, is one of the premier custom upholstery shops anywhere and they did this car too. Their take on this 1963 could be mistaken for being a 1960s original style. In actuality, it's a custom design using 1960s materials and design sense.

11 The interior of the 1953 Chevy coupe is simple and tasteful, so as not to compete for attention with the wild exterior of the car. White is a popular color for custom interiors, often contrasted with a color that matches or is of the same palette as the outside of the car. In this case, it's gold.

12 Car owners whose cars will be used strictly for show often upholster the trunk area to match the interior. That's the case with this 1953 Chevy whose interior was in the previous photo.

13 Bill Cushenbery's 1940 Ford, *El Matador*, features a dashboard based on a 1959 Chevy design, but narrowed and modified with a waterfall center and flowing into the doors and the sides. A separate floor-mounted console holds a huge tachometer. The matching steering wheel cover was popular on show cars back in the day.

14 More of *El Matador*'s interior, showing the small, none-too-comfortable seats; pod-style head restraints; and the headliner, rear package shelf, and side panels all upholstered in white tuck and roll to match the seats.

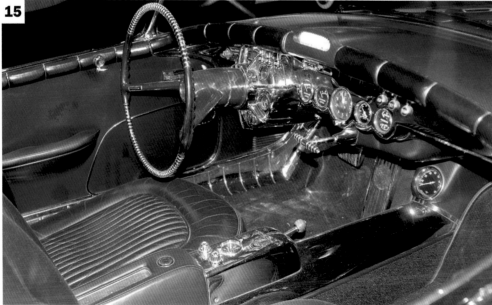

15 Hard to believe this car debuted in 1951. It's Harley Earl's GM dream car, *Le Sabre*. No, it wasn't ever called a Buick by GM. As dream cars were supposed to do, it introduced many concepts that showed up years later on production cars. An interior like this would look good in a custom, too, wouldn't it?

16 Coachcraft in California turned a 1940 Mercury into a one-of-a-kind roadster. The interior, since it was exposed, carried through the Cigarette Crème color of the outside. A snap-on tonneau covers the rear seat area.

17 and 18 Imagine what this interior must have looked like in the early 1960s when the Alexander Brothers built the *Golden Indian* 1960 Pontiac. It still looks futuristic today. The very thin bucket seats swivel and are separated by a floating console that extends to the rear between another pair of buckets. Note the chrome bases on the front seats. All-white rolled and pleated upholstery covers the seats, the instrument panel, the doors, the headliner, and the side panels and rear panel.

19

19 More of the same in the trunk of the *Golden Indian*. Since the trunks on full show customs are not used anyway, restricted space is not an issue. Often the upholsterer will effectively reduce the trunk to an upholstered box rather than trying to follow all the wheelhouse shapes, etc., in the trunk.

20 Mother of pearl isn't just for guitar pick guards anymore. The material can be purchased in sheets and applied to any flat surface, like the dashboard on this mid-1950s Ford pickup truck.

21 Rather than cut up the instrument panel and add an aftermarket stereo, Jake Moomey added a panel under the IP. It could also be used to hold air-conditioning vents and controls. The two-tone green and silver on the dashboard is a nice touch too.

22 Chevy Impala steering wheels are very popular additions to pre-1960 customs. Here's one in Lou Calasibetta's Alexander Brothers 1956 Chevy. The interior on this car is all black and gold, with pleats on the dashboard, kick panels, and even the floors. By the way, there's a third pedal barely visible on the left. This is a manual transmission car.

23 The trunk of the *Golden Chariot* 1956 Chevy is upholstered too. The car retains its spare tire, and it's placed right in the center of the trunk. The back panel is contoured around it.

24 Who says the speaker grilles have to be the same size as the speaker? In this case, the vintage-style speaker cloth has been used as a design element on the rear package tray. This is an idea that works on kick panels, doors, and consoles too.

25 Early cars had very stylish steering wheels, so it's often feasible to retain the stock wheel and incorporate it into the custom's interior design. Case in point: the 1941 Buick wheel, which has been restored. A classic wheel can often be restored for less money than it would cost to purchase a generic billet wheel that's on every common street rod.

26 Where to start on this one? The car is John Cooper's *El Tiki* built by Tom Culbertson of Indianapolis. The instrument panel is a narrowed 1956 Oldsmobile unit. The custom console has more Oldsmobile waffle-pattern metal on it. The round object at the lower right is a rare Tachrad radio. The carpet is late 1950s (think 1959 Pontiac Bonneville) silver Mylar flecked.

27 and 28 The radical custom tuck-and-roll interior in this 1958 Ford was originally done in the early 1960s by Harry Loveland. Joe Perez recently reworked it. The seats are barely recognizable as being from a Thunderbird and have purple velvet button-tufted inserts. The pleats extend over the rear package shelf. Sculpted door panels, a rear seat bar cabinet, and a Princess phone add to the period ambience. The dashboard is stock but with a tucked and rolled top. Underneath, there's a television. The stock Ford steering wheel looks customized simply by adding a bullet in the center.

29 Don't forget safety when building your early custom. For cars that didn't come with them, several companies market add-on turn signal units that look very much like the accessory ones from the 1940s and 1950s. Turn signals weren't standard equipment on all cars until 1956, so many before then didn't have the left stick.

30 through 32 Here's an interior in transition. This 1959 Edsel was formerly the author's car, bought off eBay with the blue interior as shown, a combination of aftermarket generic seat covers and original door panels, dashboard, etc. The plan was to do the interior in red and black tuck and roll, so the dashboard was painted flat black (and pinstriped by Dustin Cooper), Mexican blankets were put on the seats, and the blue headliner was spray painted (big mistake). Koch's Steering Wheels of Canyon Country, California, restored the steering wheel and Tullahoma Seat Cover of Tullahoma, Tennessee, made the door panels. A change of plans involved a black and pearl white upholstery kit from EzBoy Rod Interiors, installed by Tullahoma Seat Cover, along with black loop pile carpet and a new headliner.

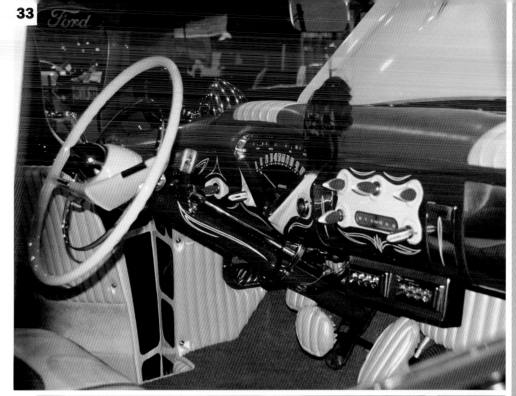

33 Like the original, the clone of the *Kopper Kart* includes lots of copper plating and rolled and pleated vinyl. A stock Chevy steering wheel sports a bullet in the center. Removable pleated covers on the pedals are for show. Car owners who drove their cars regularly put them on to cover the dirty or worn pedals.

34 The 1950s GM Motorama dream car Cadillac LeMans can serve as inspiration for a custom interior, especially for one from the mid-1950s to early 1960s era. The center stack console and instrument panel are similar to the later Corvette Sting Ray in appearance but more angular (and easier to produce as a one-off). The ribbed console could be made from a piece of luxury car trim from the late 1950s, such as a 1958 Buick Roadmaster.

35 Sometimes an unexpected splash of color can be added in an unconventional way. Here a section of Mexican blanket has been used to cover an armrest.

36 Matching laminated plastic teardrop knobs for the shifter, radio, light switch, and other locations were popular add-on custom accessories in the 1950s and early 1960s. They are available in many different sizes and colors from several sources today.

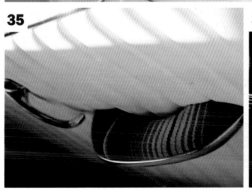

37 through 40 Geno DiPol's *Dixie Deluxe* has a custom interior by Doug Corson at Classic & Street Rod Interiors of Grand Junction, Colorado. The front seats are from a 1962 Chevy Impala SS, while the back seats came out of a 1964 Ford Thunderbird, modified to fit. Geno's roots are in New Orleans, thus the Dixie theme. Playing off the Confederate flag used as a headliner, Corson embossed stars into the seat backs between the white piping in the V-shaped areas. He did the same on the doors. That red and ivory 1955 Corvette steering wheel, restored by Koch's Steering Wheels, set the tone and color scheme for the entire car. Even the brake pedal (actually a belt buckle) continues the Dixie theme.

37

38

39

40

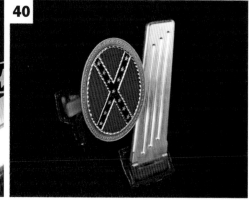

41 How easy it would be to graft this section of a 1961 Dodge instrument panel onto the dashboard of another car. It would be a real highlight of the custom's interior. It looks pretty good in the Dodge here too.

42 John D'Agostino retained the Olds steering wheel in his *Golden Star* 1957 Oldsmobile custom, but he put it on a new tilt steering column. Some customizers take out the stylish stock instrument clusters and replace them with generic round gauges in a hunk of sheet metal. D'Agostino knows better.

43 Believe it or not, this interior was done in 1962 by the famous upholsterer Eddie Martinez, and this photo was taken 46 years later. Bill Hines recently restored the *Buddha Buggy* 1959 Chevy, and the white vinyl/blue frieze interior required little more than a good cleaning. The lower part of the instrument panel is chrome plated. That big hunk on the right side is a record player.

44 When scouring swap meets for custom parts, keep in mind that in the early days, most customs were customized with updated or upmarket parts from other production cars. The horn ring on this 1940s Chevy steering wheel has "Chevrolet" cast into it and would look great on a slightly older Chevy custom.

45 Tom Culbertson's 1956 Lincoln custom, named *Loretta*, sports a gold and white vinyl interior using Thunderbird bucket seats. The importance of a comfortable interior cannot be overlooked, especially if the car is driven long distances like this one is.

46 Always keep your eyes open when plying the rows at swap meets and car shows, whether custom and rod shows or ones with stock vehicles. You'll surely come upon some neat features that can be adapted to your own next project. This chrome speaker grille and adjacent heater control panel are examples.

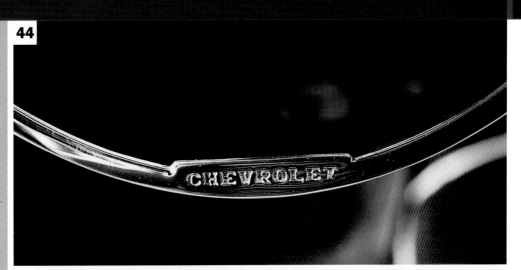

47 Too much leopard print can be overwhelmingly gaudy. This interior takes a more stylistically pleasing approach by having it as inserts in the seats only. And should the owner change his mind about the leopard accents, they could be replaced with something else relatively inexpensively.

48 Think the entire interior design through, and do not compromise on details. *Dixie Deluxe* has original-style door handles and window cranks rather than the easier to find, but ugly, chunky billet pieces some guys settle for.

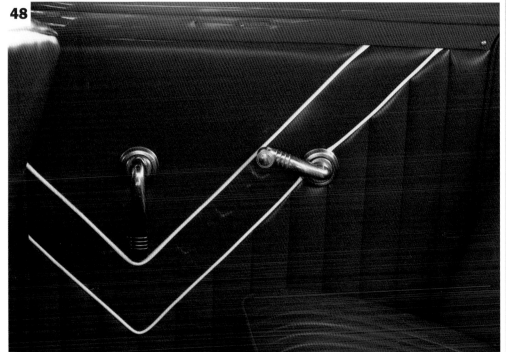

49 Not sure what car this is from, but it has some attractive features, not the least of which is that the steering wheel doesn't have any name on it, making it readily adaptable to any make of car. The identifying names have been taken off the instrument panel, too, so that makes it much more adaptable. Simple ones like this can be split and narrowed for use in narrower, older cars.

50 Old car gauges can be adapted for modern use. If they're six volt, they can be converted and, if necessary, there are companies that can rebuild them, too. That allows the use of stylish old gauges in customs, a much better choice aesthetically than resorting to generic off-the-shelf street rod gauges.

51 Sometimes standing out in a crowd of other cars requires a radical departure from the norm. This door panel is part of a nearly complete wood interior in a custom 1957 Mercury station wagon. Using different types of wood, the builder has given the interior some contrast and interest. It's not for everyone though.

52 Lots of custom car owners display their club plaques either hanging from the rear bumper or mounted in the rear window. Few could compete with the brass and neon one like this from the Auto Butchers in Los Angeles.

53 Old-style aftermarket speaker covers like this chrome one with a musical note fit well with 1950s to early 1960s custom interiors. These are available from several sources and work much better than contemporary ones from the local stereo shop.

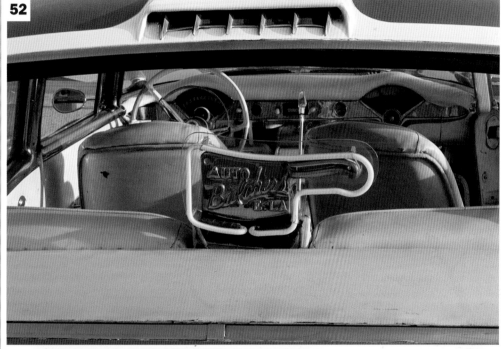

Acknowledgments

Though I would like to take credit for having taken all the photos myself, I did not do so. Approximately one-third were borrowed from my photographer and builder friends and colleagues. Here, in order of the number of photos loaned by each one, is a list of the photographers I borrowed shots from:

Anna Marco
John Jackson
Mike Basso
Jack Criswell
Bo Huff
Ian Shipley
Craig Mayes
Bobby Stewart
Mitzi Valenzuela
Michael Steven Smith
Brad Masterson
Ed Donato
Gennaro Sepe
Mark Kawakami
Roy Varga
Luigi Ciorra
Darrell Arment
Jerry Mattson
Max Grundy
Jason Mordoh
Darryl Starbird
Josh Kurpius
Mike Scott
Luke Karosi
Gary "Chopit" Fioto
Bo Bertilsson
Butch Pate
Linda Naprstek
Jeff Allison
Kai Salmio
Gene Winfield

I appreciate their friendship and generosity. You may have noticed from some of my comments in this book that I'm a little opinionated when it comes to customs. That's because I believe that customs are an art form and not everyone is an artist. Sometimes I seek second opinions from a few associates and friends whose taste and advice I respect. I would like to acknowledge their input and thank them for it. Some are included in the list of photo providers above. The others are Gordy Brown, Dave Kinnaman, Kevin Anderson, Jerry Weesner, Gary Meyers, Lou Calasibetta, Bill Dillman, Gary Brown, M.K. John, and the late Elden Titus.

Index